THE COLLEGE AWARENESS GUIDE

What Students Need to Know to Succeed in College

Bruce M. Rowe

LOS ANGELES PIERCE COLLEGE

PEARSON

Prentice Hall

Upper Saddle River, New Jersey
Columbus, Ohio

Library of Congress Cataloging-in-Publication Data

Rowe, Bruce M.
  The college awareness guide : what students need to know
to succeed in college/Bruce M. Rowe.
    p. cm.
  Includes bibliographical references and index.
  ISBN 0-13-171666-2
  1. College student orientation—United States.
  2. Academic achievement—United States. I. Title.
  LB2343.32.R678 2007
  378.1'98—dc22   2006012024

Vice President and Publisher: Jeffery W. Johnston
Executive Editor: Sande Johnson
Developmental Editor: Jennifer Gessner
Production Editor: Alexandrina Benedicto Wolf
Production Coordinator: Holcomb Hathaway
Design Coordinator: Diane C. Lorenzo
Cover Designer: Jeff Vanik
Production Manager: Pamela D. Bennett
Director of Marketing: David Gesell
Marketing Manager: Amy Judd

This book was set in Goudy by Integra. It was printed and bound by R.R. Donnelley & Sons
Company. The cover was printed by R. R. Donnelley & Sons Company.

Photo Credits: p. 6, Stockdisc; **p. 12,** BananaStock; **p. 27,** EyeWire; **p. 36,** Image 100; **p. 54,**
BananaStock; **p. 74,** Stockdisc; **p. 82,** BananaStock; **p. 98,** BananaStock; **p. 112,** PhotoDisc.

Pearson Education Ltd.   Pearson Education Australia Pty. Limited
Pearson Education Singapore Pte. Ltd.   Pearson Education North Asia Ltd.
Pearson Education Canada, Ltd.   Pearson Educación de Mexico, S.A. de C.V.
Pearson Education–Japan   Pearson Education Malaysia Pte. Ltd.

PEARSON
Prentice
Hall

10 9 8 7 6 5 4 3 2 1
ISBN 0-13-171666-2

This book is dedicated to a person
who exemplifies the success
that a returning student can attain,
my wife, Christine Louise Rowe.

Contents

1 Preparing to Go to College   1

2 Starting Out   11

3 Developing College Survival Skills   63

4 Outside the College Walls   111

APPENDIX

A Vocabulary Building   117

APPENDIX

B Additional Sources of Information   121

NOTE: Every effort has been made to provide accurate and current Internet information in this book. However, the Internet and information posted on it are constantly changing, so it is inevitable that some of the Internet addresses listed in this textbook will change.

Preface

Going to college should be an adventure filled with unlimited possibilities. However, many students feel lost and alienated in their first year of college. Those who have just graduated from high school may find college life bewilderingly different. Students returning to school after years of absence may be equally overwhelmed. Nonnative students may find their English skills inadequate. This book strives to create awareness of what students need to know about college life to succeed. I hope that this knowledge will help students enjoy their college experience.

In the past, only an elite few went to college. In 1940, under 5 percent of the U. S. population had gone to college for four years or more. Today, a majority of the U. S. population believes that a college education is valuable and should be accessible to everyone. The percentage of Americans attending college has steadily risen, especially since World War II. According to 2002 U. S. census data, 25.9 percent of Americans 25 years old or older had earned at least a bachelor's degree (see www.census.gov/Press-Release/www/releases/archives/american_community_survey_acs/001802.html). The pressure to attain higher education, combined with often inadequate high school preparation, has led to a large number of entering students without the prerequisite skills or the motivation to do well in college.

This guide is written for all types of new college students. Although this book provides general advice on numerous topics, it is not meant to be a workbook on college skills. Instead, it provides numerous sources on topics important to college students, including tutorials on college skills. Accordingly, most sections of this guide include suggested websites and/or books on a specific topic. These sources may be found within a specific discussion or at the end of a discussion. In addition, here are some good general textbooks on "surviving" in college published by Prentice Hall:

Carol Carter, Joyce Bishop, and Sarah Kravits. *Keys to Success: Building Intelligence for College, Career, and Life*, 5th ed. Upper Saddle River, NJ: Prentice Hall, 2006.

Laurie Hazard and Jean-Paul Nadeau. *Foundations for Learning.* Upper Saddle River, NJ: Prentice Hall, 2006.

Robert M. Sherfield, Rhonda J. Montgomery, and Patricia G. Moody. *Cornerstone: Building on Your Best*, 4th ed. Upper Saddle River, NJ: Prentice Hall, 2005.

I recommend that all new students thoroughly read all of the literature sent to them by the college they are about to attend, read the information in the college catalog that usually appears before the individual course descriptions, and attend all advisement sessions (orientation meetings). College counseling departments usually plan these sessions. However, individual academic departments may also have their own orientation meetings. Additionally, I recommend that students take any placement tests available even if they are not required. English, reading, and math tests are commonly offered and usually required.

Numerous websites are listed in this guide. I wish to caution readers that I cannot be responsible for the information on any of these sites. Plan to check out any claims or important information found on these sites with college personnel.

Bruce M. Rowe

Acknowledgments

I would like to thank Rita Castellano, Minnette Lenier, Mary Edith Cooper, Sandra Schulman, Thomas Smith, and Florence K. Robin (all of Pierce College) for proofreading and/or contributing information for early versions of this book. I would also like to thank my editor, Sande Johnson, and the other people from Prentice Hall who worked on this edition.

I wish to thank those who have reviewed the text and have suggested changes and additions that have strengthened it along the way: Deborah Miller, Ohio State University, Newark; Sara Connolly; Sally Barton Dingee, Monroe Community College; Paul E. Panek, Ohio State University, Newark; Harry Rosemond, Ventura College; Reba Rowe Lewis, Virginia Polytechnic University; David Filak, Joliet Junior College; Patricia Russ, Vista College; Brent Vulcano, St. Mary's University; Charlie Richardson, Oakland Community College; and Arlene Jorgensen, Central Arizona College.

I would like to thank my wife, Christine L. Rowe, who proofread the manuscript and made numerous valuable suggestions.

Finally, I would like to thank my sons, Aaron Rowe and Andrew Rowe, who were attending college while I was writing this text and shared their experiences with me. I asked my wife and sons, "If you had to give one or two suggestions to entering freshmen, what would they be?" Christine said that each two-year college freshman should see a counselor, should make sure that the classes that he or she will be taking at the community college will transfer to the four-year schools to which the student intends to apply, and should take classes in the proper sequence. Aaron suggested that most students take a light load of classes at first to test their skills and to avoid feeling overwhelmed. And Andrew warns against procrastination. He suggests that students do not leave assignments or applying for scholarships, housing, or other school-related activities until the last minute.

Preparing to Go to College

This guide is geared toward both high school juniors and seniors and college freshmen. If you are already in college, some parts of this first section might not apply to you unless you will be applying to another college. For instance, many community college students will apply to four-year universities.

A Checklist of Things to Do

When you are applying to colleges, you need to take certain steps:

_____ Carefully explore the possible choices of schools available to you (see "Choosing a College" in this chapter).

_____ After you have been accepted to a college, apply for financial aid by the appropriate deadlines (see "Obtaining Financial Support" in Chapter 2).

_____ If you are going to be living away from home, apply for housing (see "Choosing a Place to Live" in this chapter).

_____ Inform the school that you intend to go to that you accept its invitation to attend. Officially decline offers to attend colleges that accepted you but that you will not be attending.

_____ Verify when fees for tuition, housing, parking permits, and so on are due or when deposits are due. Find out if fees or deposits are required for phones, cable TV, Internet access, and other utilities.

_____ Get names of potential roommates and contact them. You might decide that you want to request a change of roommate or roommates. You might also want to share the responsibilities of what to bring to your room, such as a television and various items of furniture.

_____ Confirm move-in dates and the rules for moving into the residence hall. Find out if your school allows microwave ovens or other electrical appliances in residence hall rooms.

_____ Make sure you know the dates to apply for classes. If you miss a registration date, you might have to wait until you are given another date. By that time classes could be closed.

_____ Check your school email. Frequently, colleges use school email for important official communications with students.

_____ Get your textbooks early if possible. However, first refer to "Textbooks" in Chapter 2.

_____ Attend all school orientation meetings and appointments with counselors.

_____ Get to know the neighborhood surrounding your school. Find the locations of restaurants, banks, retail stores, places of entertainment, and other places in the neighborhood that might be important to you.

Choosing a College

Although most who are reading this book are already attending a college or university, an overview of what different types of colleges have to offer might be valuable for some students. In addition, some students may wish to reevaluate their choice of school because of disenchantment with the social environment, educational offerings, or cost of their current location. A change in place of residence may force a change in school as well.

There are several types of postsecondary educational institutions—technical/vocational schools, community colleges, state colleges, and universities.

Technical/Vocational Schools

Technical or vocational schools usually offer programs in specific skills such as nursing, plumbing, hotel management, auto mechanics, computer repair and programming, and landscape design. These programs are designed for job training, and the course of study may take anywhere from weeks to years.

Community Colleges

Many community colleges also offer vocational programs. In addition, community colleges offer the first two years of a four-year college education and provide a broad liberal arts background. That is to say, they offer courses in most academic areas and they require liberal arts students to take a sampling of courses from a number of areas such as history, English, biology, art, humanities, and earth sciences. The liberal arts program is generally not geared toward employment but toward transfer to a four-year college or university.

Community colleges often have an "open-door" policy that allows them to accept almost anyone who applies. For this reason, the degree of academic preparation of students in any specific class may range from remedial to exceptional.

Compared with four-year schools, community colleges have the following advantages:

1. **Community colleges are likely to be much less expensive than four-year schools.** According to The College Board, for the 2004–2005 school year, the average cost for a full year of tuition at a community college in the United States was $2,076. In some states, such as California, at a cost of $780, annual community college tuition (actually called fees) is less than half that. The average cost of tuition in an American public four-year school was $5,132 for the 2004–2005 school year. At an average of $20,082, private American colleges charge almost four times that of public institutions.

In 2005, attending a community college for the first two years of a four-year education could save an average of $6,048 in tuition and fees and even much more, depending on the college options available. As we will see below, attending a community college first and then transferring to a four-year school could result in other savings. However, the actual situation is more complicated than the aforementioned calculations, because the amount of financial aid a student might receive will affect the actual cost of the education. Grants and aid might lessen the cost of an education, whereas loans might increase costs because of interest payments.

2. **Community colleges are conveniently located.** Most people who go to community colleges live in the general area of the college. This can be convenient for a number of reasons. First, a person who has a job can

continue to work at that job while going to college. Second, community college students can take as few classes as they wish, thus enabling them to manage comfortably their work and school time. Third, it is very difficult for most people to work long hours and also be a full-time student at a four-year institution. Although a four-year school might be close to home, it is likely that a community college is also close to home. If this is the case, you would not have to move and pay college housing costs. According to The College Board, the average college housing costs in the 2004–2005 academic year were about $6,222.

3. **Instructors tend to be student oriented.** Because the instructor's main job at a community college is teaching (not doing research), he or she may choose to focus more attention on students than do some university professors. Of course, this is an extreme generalization. Some professors at four-year institutions are very student oriented and some instructors at community colleges may pay little attention to student needs.

4. **Classes at community colleges often are smaller than at four-year institutions.** Whereas an introductory freshman class at a community college is likely to have fewer than 50 students, the same course at some four-year schools might have hundreds of students gathered in a large lecture hall.

5. **A community college may offer more of a personal feeling and a more relaxed environment than that found at universities, especially large universities.**

One limitation of community colleges is that they only offer the first two years of a four-year education. The highest degree that one can attain at a community college is an associate's degree such as Associate of Arts or Associate of Science. At a four-year school, one can achieve a bachelor's, and possibly a master's and/or a doctor's degree.

Four-Year Colleges and Universities

In addition to full-degree programs, advantages of a four-year school are as follows:

1. **Faculty involvement and dedication.** The faculty members may be more actively involved in the subjects that they teach, and their enthusiasm for their research and other activities having to do with their subject area can be inspiring to students.

2. **The atmosphere may appear more collegiate and scholarly.** Because more students who attend a four-year institution live on campus or in nearby campus college housing, and more of these students are full-time than at a typical community college, their lives are more involved with a campus lifestyle. They may attend more college-sponsored activities and study and socialize with more students than the average community college student.

3. **The average degree of advanced preparation for college courses may be greater for students admitted to a four-year institution than to a community college.** This might translate to faster-paced courses in which the instructor can delve into more advanced data and concepts without losing a major portion of the class.

4. **The school may offer more courses.** Within a major, even at the freshman and sophomore levels, a four-year school may have a much broader offering of courses.

5. **The facilities may be better.** Libraries may be bigger, labs may be better equipped, and services such as student medical facilities may be available.

6. **A student at a four-year school may have the opportunity to take several classes from a favorite professor.** For example, a professor might teach both lower-division (freshman and sophomore) and upper-division (junior and senior) classes.

7. **A four-year school may offer better experiences and continuity compared with a two-year school.** For instance, at a four-year school one might be able to work in a lab, take on another student job, or work for a student organization and develop long-term friendships more easily than at a two-year school. It may be easier to develop a complex network of relationships that might be important assets for getting into a graduate program or getting a job.

This comparison of the advantages of community colleges and four-year schools is very general. A large university may provide all of the advantages listed for four-year schools, and a small one might be more like a community college in some ways. There is no substitute for exploring in person the campus or campuses that you wish to attend. If you have a specific major in mind, see what each college offers. Do not make your choice solely on the basis of geographic proximity or college costs. In relationship to cost, sometimes the colleges that are the most expensive give large grants and

Students who attend a four-year college, who are likely to live on or near campus, may be more involved with a campus lifestyle.

scholarships to students with high grade point averages, special skills, or other qualifications.

As mentioned, a major step in choosing a college is visiting it. When you visit a college you can see the facilities and talk to faculty, staff, and students. You can get the "lay of the land." Although I have listed several sources below that describe and even rank colleges and universities, such rankings should be taken for what they are. They tend to rank schools on the basis of the average SAT or ACT scores of the students they accepted, acceptance-rejection ratios of their applicants, financial status of the institution, prestige of their faculty, and other factors that may have little relevance to an individual student with individual needs. It is therefore important to go to open houses (college days) or make your own arrangements to visit the colleges that you are considering.

The most current editions of the following books, which are available at many libraries, contain a variety of information on individual colleges and provide a ranking of the colleges based on a number of different criteria, including the ones just discussed:

The College Blue Book, New York: Macmillan. This multivolume set of books provides general information about colleges as well as information on scholarships, fellowships, grants, degrees offered, and occupational education.

Undergraduate Guide: Two Year Colleges, Lawrenceville, NJ: Peterson.

Peterson's Complete Guide to Colleges, Lawrenceville, NJ: Peterson.

Lovejoy's College Guide, New York: Monarch Press.

You may also search for information about colleges on the Internet. Here are some good websites:

www.collegenet.com

www.collegeboard.com

www.collegeview.com

www.princetonreview.com

www.petersons.com

www.usnews.com

Individual college catalogs can be requested by writing directly to colleges or visiting the college website; catalogs may also be found at college or other large libraries.

Choosing a Place to Live

As mentioned in the previous section, living at home might save an average of more than $6,000 a year; that would be at least $24,000 over four years! And the cost of housing rises each year. Of course, living at home is not an option for many students. For others, living on campus might be just what they need for a variety of reasons. The decision to live on campus may not always be yours or your parents', because college housing is limited at many universities. In fact, on-campus housing can be very difficult to get at some universities. In many cases, there is a lottery for the available spots.

Some colleges and universities require new students to spend at least the first year on campus living in campus residence halls (*residence hall* is becoming the preferred term instead of *dorm* or *dormitory*). There are several reasons for this requirement. Living on campus for at least the freshman year helps students, especially those who have never been away from home for any length of time, to get used to living on their own in a transitional way. By living in campus housing, students are separated from their parents and friends back home, but they are also taken care of in a number of ways. Dining halls provide food, some medical services are available, potential friends are nearby, and maid service is even available at some residence halls. After a year in student housing, students might be better prepared to live in off-campus housing. Living on campus also provides students with a wide range of social possibilities including meeting a large number and diversity of people in various academic and social contexts potentially every waking hour. Students living on campus are also more likely to meet informally with instructors and to attend more college-sponsored events. Residence halls are usually on the college campus itself or very close by, so students are close enough to their classes to walk or bike to them. Some larger campuses provide free bus service around the campus. In addition, numerous studies have shown that students who live on campus compared with those who live off campus are more likely to graduate, are more satisfied with their college experience, and on average earn better grades (see Ernest T. Pascarella and Patrick T. Terenzini, *How College Affects Students: A Third Decade of Research*, 2nd rev. ed. New York: Jossey-Bass, 2005).

Living in student housing on campus also has disadvantages. You could be paired with a student who is completely incompatible with you. For example, your roommate might enjoy partying all the time whereas you might be a serious student, or your roommate might be a "night person" whereas you might prefer to turn in early. If this is the case, immediately ask to be reassigned to a different room. In addition, residence hall rooms are usually very small and can be very crowded, allowing little privacy.

Most college advisors see more advantages than disadvantages to immersing oneself, at least for a year or so, in the total experience of being away from home in a college or university environment. In a large sense, this immersion might be one of the more valuable parts of your college education and experience.

Students can often request different types of residence halls and to be paired with a specific person. This usually has to be done when applying for a residence hall or at some other specific time. Some universities have a wide range of types of college housing; others are limited. Here are some possibilities:

1. **Single-sex residence halls.** Some colleges and universities require students to be in single-sex residence halls. Years ago, this was the rule for most universities. Today, it might be an option or required for at least the freshman year. Visits by people of the opposite sex may be prohibited or restricted in various ways.

2. **Theme housing.** Many larger universities offer special residence halls or at least designate different floors in residence halls for students with different social or academic interests. There may be residence halls for specific areas of study such as art, science, or English. There might be specific college housing for international students or returning students. And there are often different residence halls for undergraduate and graduate students. Some colleges even offer housing that is supposed to be especially quiet or that has early "lights off" rules.

3. **Drug-free residence halls.** Some universities offer housing that is supposed to be free of smoking and alcohol. Of course, all residence halls are supposed to be free of illegal drugs. Alcohol and other types of drug abuse is a big problem on American campuses. In 2002, alcohol abuse led to about 1,400 deaths and about 500,000 injuries on these campuses. Drunken students were also responsible for nearly 700,000 acts of violence and a number of other problems including academic difficulties. Substance-free residence halls will not completely insulate students from the peer pressures to drink excessively or take drugs, but offering this housing is a step toward that end. Some universities impose severe penalties for students who get caught using banned substances in these residence halls.

4. **Types of residence hall rooms.** Most students who stay in a college residence hall have a roommate. It is unlikely that a college would give a single room to a first-year student, unless there were extenuating circumstances. However, a student might request a private room because the student believes that he or she might have problems studying with a roommate present or the student may simply not be socially oriented. A private room will usually cost more than a shared one.

Students who are disabled might need a private room for a variety of reasons, and the university might agree with these reasons and therefore grant the request. These students should contact the director of campus housing as soon as they have sent in their letter of acceptance, and should register with the special services office of their college. People in that office can sometimes help obtain a private room for such students. Students who are disabled need to consider their needs and investigate how each college can satisfy those needs.

In addition to single and double rooms, some universities offer suites. A suite consists of two or more bedrooms and usually a common room. This is a good option for many students. They can go into their bedroom if they wish to be alone or get some sleep while other students study or socialize in the common room. In addition, the common room allows friends to sleep over more easily because it is larger than a closet-sized room. Suites also provide an environment that helps a group of people to develop close ties and share expenses.

There are many off-campus living options. For example, you may have relatives or friends who live in the area of the school. If you are compatible with them you could make arrangements to stay with them. In addition, there may be opportunities to house-sit for people who will be away for an extended period of time. Some of the more common off-campus housing options are living in university-owned apartments, privately owned apartments, or co-ops of various types; renting a house (usually with other students sharing the rent) or a room in someone's house; or even buying a house. Buying a house jointly with friends or with the help of parents could be a good option. If you are going to be at a school for four or more years, this option could be a good investment, because you could sell the house for a profit when you graduate. However, before embarking on such a venture, you need to be sure you have the financial resources to do this and thoroughly investigate the potential risks involved.

Make sure you consult with your college's housing department about any questions you have. It probably will have both printed and Internet information on housing options and availability in the area of your school.

Usually a college will have a community housing website. Following are some of the many Internet sites that might help you find a roommate or satisfy other housing needs. Be cautious of any service that asks you for up-front service fees.

RoommateNation.com at www.roommatenation.com

Webroomz at www.webroomz.com

RoommateLocator at www.roommatelocator.com

College Sublease at www.collegesublease.com

College Roommate Search at www.college-roommates.com

College-Apartmentsonet at www.college-apartments.net

These articles discuss living away from home:

"Your First Year Away From Home" (from the University of California, Santa Barbara) at http://kiosk.ucsb.edu/HousingOptions/Index.asp?page=housingoptions (or type *"Housing Options" "UCSB"* into a search engine)

"Solutions to Homesickness" (Type *"Solutions to Homesickness" "East Carolina University"* into a search engine)

Starting Out

The Importance of a Positive Attitude

Most people aspire to succeed in college. Why, then, does success sometimes elude them? It is true that people are born with different potentials, giving some an initial advantage over others. People also differ in how they were treated as children and young adults, so those with nurturing parents and teachers may enter college with a better self-image and more developed skills than those brought up in a nonsupportive environment. As a result, one student may learn easily what another struggles to learn; however, that disparity need not doom the latter student to low levels of performance. As Thomas Alva Edison observed: "Genius is 1 percent inspiration and 99 percent perspiration." Without effort, even the most gifted student is likely to fail. On the other hand, extra effort can make up for almost any initial disadvantage. This book is intended to guide that effort.

The first step to success in college is to make a realistic assessment of one's skills and goals. The next is to devise a good plan of attack. The final step is to work hard in implementing that plan. Essential to all these steps is a positive attitude. Optimism is a great motivator, and motivation is the parent of effort. One cannot set goals in a pessimistic frame of mind, much less actually accomplish them.

One way to maintain optimism is to associate with friends who are enthusiastic, have a conquering attitude, and are goal oriented. Both negative and positive attitudes can be contagious. Another aid to a positive attitude is to become involved in what you are studying. Replace "Do I have to read this whole chapter?" with "What else can I find to read on this subject?" This is part of an active approach to life, one in which you choose your classes,

Become involved in what you are studying to help achieve a positive attitude.

your friends, your daily activities, and even your daily attitude, rather than passively accept whatever comes along.

Being motivated is important for success. Motivation is often driven by intrinsic factors such as having a positive attitude toward life and being a goal-oriented person. But there are extrinsic factors as well. In addition to the things we have already discussed, here are other important actions you can take to maintain or increase your level of motivation: To reduce frustration, manage your time and plan out your activities (see "Time Management" in Chapter 3). Manage your stress (see "Stress Management" in Chapter 3), get enough sleep and eat well, and seek help if you suffer from depressive or other emotional disorders (see "Seeing a Counselor or an Advisor" and "Pitfalls of College Life" in this chapter). Choose your courses and instructors carefully (see "Choosing Classes" and "Choosing Instructors" in this chapter). Finally, set realistic goals and work toward those goals, and make a realistic assessment of your abilities (see the next section). Perhaps nothing demotivates people more than failure. This book aims to help you succeed in college. Check out these resources:

Finding the Right Solution at www.campusblues.com/studentoflife_3.asp

University of Minnesota Duluth's Handbook at www.d.umn.edu/student/loon/acad/strat/motivate.html

Lakeland Community College Counseling Center's Guidelines for Academic Success. This site offers much good advice, including a section on motivation, at www.lakelandcc.edu/ADMISSIO/COUNSEL/cc_asc.htm

Setting Realistic Goals

Patience may be the key ingredient to your success. For example, if your reading skills are low, allow time to improve them before attempting courses that require a high level of these skills. Many colleges offer credit-bearing reading courses. If you cannot write well, take a writing course. If your mathematics skills are weak, find out if your major requires courses that involve math. If it does, take some introductory math courses to prepare yourself. If necessary, find out where you can obtain tutoring. In other words, set yourself up for success, not for failure.

Because self-esteem is so important to success, beware of damaging it by having to drop out of a too difficult course or by earning a low grade in that course because you were not ready to tackle it. Taking courses in which you can earn good grades (short-term goals) will create motivation and momentum to proceed toward your long-term goals—succeeding in more difficult courses and, ultimately, obtaining a degree and a good job. However, if you have worked hard in a class and received a passing grade—even if that grade is lower than what you had expected or wished for—take pride in the fact that you finished the course.

It is also important to take courses in the recommended order. For instance, do not take an upper-division (junior- or senior-level) course in a subject before you take the lower-division (freshman and sophomore) prerequisites. Or, at least, discuss this possibility with a counselor or the instructor teaching the upper-division class.

Choose a realistic course load. Many first-time college students overload themselves with work (see Exhibit 2.1). A college on a semester system with a fall and spring semester might have a short session between the two regular semesters, called an intersession. It is also common for students who attend summer school or an intersession to take too many courses or courses that are too difficult. The six weeks or shorter periods of time of the usual summer or

EXHIBIT 2.1	Hours spent per week on schoolwork based on number of units attempted.

NUMBER OF UNITS OR CREDITS	HOURS IN CLASS	AVERAGE HOURS OF HOMEWORK	TOTAL HOURS
3	3	9	12
6	6	18	24
9	9	27	36
12	12	36	48
15	15	45	60

intersession go by very quickly. Other parts of this guide include suggestions on how to avoid "overload." Students would be wise to follow the tortoise's example in the fable "The Tortoise and the Hare": "Slow and steady wins the race."

Choosing a Major and a Career

Nationally, between 20 and 40 percent of freshmen entering college have not chosen a major. Between 75 and 80 percent of students change their major at least once. The advantage of having chosen a major early in your college years is that you can focus on satisfying the requirements for that major. Not knowing what to major in or changing majors can extend the time it takes you to complete your degree. However, this is not always the case, because a student who enters college not knowing what to major in might spend the first year or two taking general education courses.

One of the great advantages of going to a four-year liberal arts college or a community college is the size of the academic menu. That is, there are so many subjects to choose from that one can experiment (see "Why Do I Have to Take This Course? The Goals of Liberal Studies" in this chapter). A high school graduate has not necessarily been exposed to a large array of different areas of study and potential careers. The "undecided major" can start out by taking courses that satisfy general graduation requirements for all students. While taking these general education classes the student might find a field that he or she never imagined would have been so exciting.

On the website Quintessential Careers, Randall S. Hansen lists six things you should consider when choosing a major and a future career (www.quintcareers.com/choosing_major.html):

1. Ask yourself, "What excites me?"
2. Assess what you are good at.
3. Ask yourself, "What do I want to get out of a job other than a salary?"
4. Explore what types of careers you might have with a specific major.
5. When you settle on a possible career, assess the reality of fulfilling the requirements for that career.
6. After you have decided on what your career aspirations are, decide what major or majors will lead to that career.

Hansen's website explores in detail each of these six points.

Your school's career center, assessment center, and various counseling services can help you with testing and counseling on your interests and abilities. In addition, many schools allow students to major in more than one field and also to minor in a field. Explore the advantages and disadvantages of multiple majors with a college counselor. The following resources provide majors and the types of jobs and careers that you might qualify for with those majors as well as other career information:

University of California, Berkeley's Career Center at
http://career.berkeley.edu/Major/Major.stm

University of North Carolina Wilmington's Career Services at
www.uncw.edu/stuaff/career/majors/index.htm

The Princeton Review at
www.princetonreview.com/college/research/majors/majorSearch.asp

CollegeBoard.com's "Choosing Your College Major" at
www.collegeboard.com/article/0,3868,4-24-0-468,00.html

CoolJobs.com at www.cooljobs.com

The Catalog and Schedule of Classes

Be certain to familiarize yourself thoroughly with your college's catalog. Always use the most recent catalog, because graduation and transfer requirements as well as other important information may change frequently. Double-check essential information from the catalog with your academic advisor, including course descriptions (see Exhibit 2.2).

EXHIBIT 2.2	Catalog description.

With the assistance of a counselor, make sure you understand the prerequisite requirements of your courses, the transferability of these courses, and other details about the courses that you are taking. In the section of the catalog descriptions from a California community college presented here, each entry describes a class and tells how many semester units the course is worth (the number in parentheses), how many of the units are for the lecture part of the course and how many are for lab (when relevant), whether it is (in this case) transferable to the University of California (UC) and/or the California State University (CSU) systems, and whether the course can be repeated (e.g., field archaeology can be repeated once).

ANTHROPOLOGY

101 Human Biological Evolution   (3)
UC:CSU (CAN ANTH 2)   lecture 3 hours

May be offered as an honors section.

Explores the field of physical anthropology emphasizing the evolution of the human species. Topics include human heredity, mechanisms of evolutionary change, human variation, and the reconstruction of human evolutionary history through the study of the fossil record and the study of our closest biological relatives, the living monkeys and apes. The philosophy of science and scientific method serve as foundations for this course.

102 Human Ways of Life: Cultural Anthropology (3)
UC:CSU (CAN ANTH 4)   lecture 3 hours

May be offered as an honors section.

Presents a broad survey of human culture including the study of human society, language, religion, political and economic organization, with examples drawn from contemporary preliterate, peasant, and urban societies.

104 Human Language and Communication   (3)
UC:CSU   lecture 3 hours

Same as Linguistics 1. Credit not given for both.

Surveys the great variety of ways humans communicate, both verbally and non-verbally. The course focuses on the structure, function, and history of language, with selections on the sociology and psychology of language, language learning, and the origins and evolution of language.

105 Prehistoric Peoples   (3)
UC:CSU   lecture 3 hours

Surveys world prehistory from the earliest evidence of the origin of culture to the development of urbanization. The course examines the prehistoric process and sequence for various parts of the world, including Europe, the Americas, Africa, and Asia.

106 Introduction to Archaeology   (4)
UC:CSU   lecture 3 hours, laboratory 2 hours

May be offered as modules 106A (lecture 3 hours, 3 units) and 106B (laboratory 2 hours, 1 unit).

Introduces students to the field of modern scientific archaeology. Lecture outlines methods traditionally used by archaeologists and critiques these in light of current archaeological objectives. Techniques for describing and classifying artifacts are discussed, as are strategies for explaining culture change. Laboratory exercises focus on analysis and interpretation of maps, soils, remote sensing imagery, and actual archaeological remains.

113 Field Archaeology   (3)
CSU - RPT 1   lecture 1 hour, laboratory 6 hours

Normally offered in the Spring semester only.

Presents an introduction to the theory and method of field work in archaeology. This is a class in archaeological excavation and related data gathering methods. The course emphasizes field techniques through actual student participation in excavation, survey and related field methods.

Examine the course descriptions, noting any prerequisites. Check to see if the course is transferable to other colleges and universities, and ensure that it fulfills the requirements of your general education, vocational, or other program needs—a list of courses that fulfill various program requirements can be found in the catalog. If the catalog does not supply an adequately detailed description, seek out the instructor who teaches the course and discuss any questions you may have. If the specific instructor for a course is not available, check with a departmental advisor, a department chairperson, or an acade-mic counselor. If possible, do this before the start of the semester.

Even if no official prerequisites are listed for a course, attempt to evaluate whether you have the reading, language, mathematical, note-taking, or other skills needed to succeed in it. At the college where I teach, the overall rate per class of students who did not successfully complete my class (those who dropped the class or got a grade below C) in the spring semester of 2004 was 32.1 percent. In some departments it was considerably greater. A lack of unofficial prerequisites is a leading cause. If you have doubts about your ability to succeed in a class, discuss them with the instructor or a counselor. This will help you to avoid wasting time in classes that you will eventually need to drop.

The catalog lists general information about student conduct, academic standards, important deadline dates, degree and certificate requirements, specific course descriptions, repeating courses, credit by examination, awards and scholarships, grading, and the consequences of incomplete grades. You can also find out about student services such as counseling, financial aid, health services, employment, housing, and tutors. In addition, the catalog is a good place to begin finding out about extracurricular activities such as clubs and student organizations.

By studying the area of the college catalog that discusses your major (and minor, if you have one) you can learn the number of courses required, the specific classes required, and sometimes, when a course is taught. For example, some courses might only be taught once a year.

The schedule of classes is published for each term (semester or quarter). It might repeat some of the information in the catalog. However, its main function is to give the time and location of each class that is being taught in a specific term. It may also give transfer information and list prerequisites, as well as provide the dates for final exams (see Exhibit 2.3).

Study the table of contents of both the catalog and schedule of classes as well as any general information at the front and back of those books. You will discover resources available to you and information about your college's offerings and student environment that you most likely did not know.

EXHIBIT 2.3	Sample of a schedule of classes.

This small segment of a schedule of classes gives information on the time(s) and day(s) that a class is offered, how many units the course is worth, transfer information, special requirements for the class, contact information, and other details about the class.

BIOLOGY

(See also Anatomy, Microbiology, Oceanography, and Physiology.)

Life Science Department Chair: Dr. James Rikel   Phone: 719-6465   Office: LS 1715
Faculty Advisor: Lyn Koller   Phone: 710-4138

STUDENTS WHO FAIL TO ATTEND THE FIRST CLASS MEETING MAY FORFEIT THEIR PLACE IN CLASS.

BIOLOGY 3 Introduction to Biology (UC:CSU)   4 units

Closed to students who have completed Biology 6.

Note: Biology 10 also fulfills the IGETC and Cal State Certified Plan requirement.

Note: Students must bring their own headphones to the first laboratory meeting. Headphones are available for purchase in the Student Store.

Note: Lab TBA hours consist of three hours of open-entry, self-paced laboratory to be completed between the hours of 9 a.m. and 5:00 p.m. Monday; 8:00 a.m. and 5:00 p.m. Tuesday, Wednesday, and Thursday; 8:00 a.m. and 12:00, Friday.

| 0184 | Lec | 8:00–9:25 | TTh | K L | Kubach | LS1728 |
| | Lab | 3 hrs 10 min | TBA | | Staff | TLC1600 |

| 0185 | Lec | 8:00–9:25 | TTh | P A | Farris | LS1700 |
| | Lab | 3 hrs 10 min | TBA | | Staff | TLC1600 |

Supplemental Instruction will be provided for students who enroll in this class.

| 0186 | Lec | 9:35–11:00 | MW | E M | Koller | LS1700 |
| | Lab | 3 hrs 10 min | TBA | | Staff | TLC1600 |

The College Website and University Email Accounts

Depending on the sophistication of the college website, it might allow you to find virtually any information about your college. It might include all of the information that is in written form in the catalog and schedule of classes. In fact, it might offer even more detailed and up-to-date information about each of the school's academic programs. It will have links to instructors' web pages and email. It might include information on job and research opportunities as well as financial aid and all other programs and services at the college. The site may allow you to register, add, drop, and change classes; access your transcripts; and review your financial accounts in relationship to school fees. You will be able to search the library catalog, reserve and renew books, and access electronic databases. The college website is likely to include college news and events, such as special lectures, concerts, sports events, travel opportunities, and other things of potential interest to you.

Exhibit 2.4 is an example of the home page of a college website. Each college will organize its page differently, but notice that the web page illustrated has a list of general categories along the top of the page, such as "Home," "Students," "Faculty," "Staff," and "Departments and Directories." On this website, when you click on any one of these categories, a new page will appear with a menu to the left (as shown in Exhibit 2.4). Then, clicking on any of those items will lead you to additional choices. Most college websites also include a search engine for the site and/or a site map. You can look for specific information by using these features.

Most universities provide email accounts to their students. Check the policy of your school on the use of such accounts. In many cases, students are expected to check these accounts often and to respond quickly to emails sent to them by the university. Colleges and universities often use these email accounts to send information on such things as registration, student financial accounts, college and department events, and other important college business. Often these email accounts can be linked to other personal email accounts the student might have.

College Bulletins, Newspapers, and Flyers

College bulletins, newspapers, and flyers (posted on bulletin boards or on walls or read by instructors) provide up-to-the-minute information. Bulletins might be posted in classrooms or be available at other

EXHIBIT 2.4   An example of a college web page.

Every college website will be different. However, most will have similar features. Carefully examine your college's website and experiment by clicking on different links.

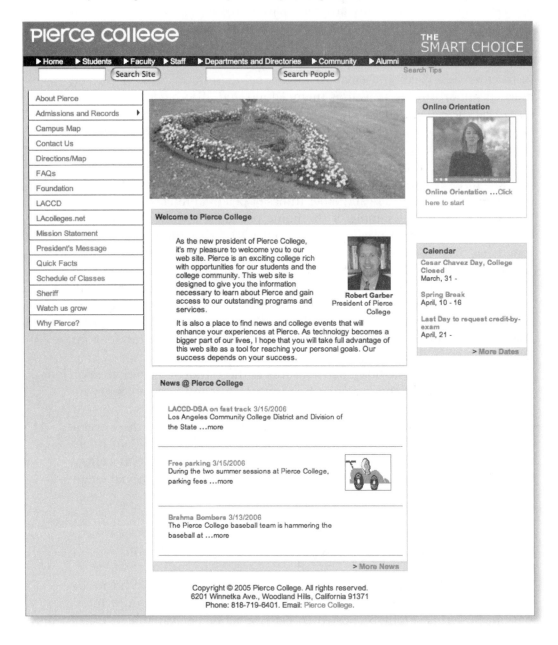

places on campus or be on the college website. Exhibit 2.5 is a segment of a weekly bulletin from my college.

Most colleges and universities also have their own newspaper. The newspaper might list and report on current events; profile professors, students, and staff; provide stories about the college and surrounding neighborhood, and have advertisements and coupons. Most important, the student newspaper offers an opportunity for students to express their ideas and opinions about the school and world events. In addition to columns by student members of the newspaper staff, any student can write a letter to the editor. Many of the features of the newspaper may also be available on the college website. In fact, the entire newspaper, in addition to being available in paper form, might be posted on the college website. Many college newspapers are also available on a site called College Newspapers Online at www.studyworld.com/college_newspapers_online.htm.

Information that you may or may not find from other sources might be found on flyers (notices) posted around campus. For example, flyers might advertise club events, lectures and discussions, and a whole range of other campus happenings. Flyers or ads also allow students to reach other students for various purposes such as selling textbooks. Find out if your college has a policy against tacking up notices, or if it allows doing so only in designated areas. Be careful about violating these rules; your name and other personal information might be on the flyer, which will allow you to be tracked and disciplined for violating school policy.

Blogs and Electronic Bulletin Boards

The term *blog* is a clipped form for weblog. Blogs started out mostly as personal journals or diaries but are now used for a variety of purposes. In addition to personal diaries, some instructors create class blogs to generate interest in a class and to motivate students. To find out more about blogs, see the site called The College Site: Students.com at www.blogs.student.com.

An electronic bulletin or message board is an Internet resource that allows a person to place information on a site in order to advertise or announce various things. For instance, there are job bulletin boards and housing bulletin boards. A search of a housing bulletin board might result in a student finding a room or roommate. Electronic bulletin boards are also used as a part of some online courses. Your college website might list various electronic bulletin boards that are of interest to students.

EXHIBIT 2.5   An example of a college weekly bulletin.

Bulletins, which are usually available on the college website, will keep you current on events at your school and various opportunities for such things as newly announced scholarships, internships, and a variety of college programs.

Weekly Bulletin

MAY 30, 2005

EVENTS OF THE WEEK

The first day of applications for the summer 2005.

Summer Registration: Summer registration is under way for Pierce students. Continuing Pierce students have first priority in registration for summer and fall. Appointment dates and times for both summer and fall were mailed to all continuing students several weeks ago. Check the Pierce website (www.piercecollege.edu) or the STEP telephone registration system (988-2222) if you have forgotten your appointment date and time.

ANNOUNCEMENTS

Students can now schedule appointments with visiting college reps online through the Internet by accessing the Transfer Center web page at www.piercecollege.com/students/transfer. Click on Schedule a Rep Visit to make your appointment. Students must have an e-mail address to receive confirmation of their appointment. Stop by the Transfer Center if you need further assistance (Administration Bldg., Room 1004).

The Pierce College GAIN/Cal WORKS Program is a campus-based service for students receiving cash public assistance for themselves and at least one child under the age of eighteen years. Benefits include free books and supplies, free child care, a transportation stipend and program-provided assistance and advocacy working with CalWORKS (public assistance), GAIN (welfare-to-work) and the Child Care Resource Center (CCRC). Referrals

to on- and off-campus medical, counseling and legal resources are provided. For more information, please call (818) 719-6400, or stop by BUNG 0327 Monday–Thursday, 8:30 a.m. to 4:30 p.m.

The Learning Center provides services to enhance student success in the classroom. All services are free to currently enrolled Pierce College students; however, there is a printing fee ($3 minimum).

Services include:

Tutoring Program (RM 035, next to cafeteria): TLC tutoring program offers free individual and/or group tutoring in a variety of subject areas. Students must make appointments in advance; appointments are 30 minutes in length. Walk-ins will be seen only if tutors are available, on a first-come, first-served basis.

Hours: Monday–Thursday 8 am–7 pm
          Friday 8 am–2 pm, Saturday—closed

Computer Labs (Rooms 1604 and 1613): 100 computer stations are available for student use. Students may utilize word processing for class-related work, access the Internet, or take advantage of computer-assisted instructional programs. Students will need to purchase a print card from the bookstore in order to print documents.

Hours: Monday–Thursday 8 am–10 pm
          Friday 8 am–2 pm, Saturday 10 am–4 pm

Choosing Classes

nless you are in a program with a predetermined sequence of classes, your success might depend on how well you choose your classes and their sequence. Seek the advice of department chairpersons and advisors, instructors of classes you are considering, and students who have taken those classes. Your current instructors are often delighted to recommend an additional course in their respective areas.

Make a *realistic* assessment of your skills. See counselors, go to study skills centers, and take the placement tests even when they are not required. Placement (or assessment) tests are designed to help you make rational predictions about your possible success in a course. Most schools will not allow you to enroll in any classes until all required assessment tests are taken.

Taking the time to evaluate your level of knowledge, understanding, and skills before you start a sequence of courses will save time later and perhaps also save money (fees for a course you had to drop, textbook costs, and so on). For example, if you are weak in math, take a math class before tackling a math class that requires mathematical sophistication. Surprisingly, many students neglect this commonsense approach. For instance, I teach a class at the introductory level on physical anthropology. This is not a math class, yet in the section on human genetics basic probability theory and some algebra are applied to solving genetics problems. Although these concepts are explained in class, those students who are weak in math sometimes wind up dropping the class.

Additionally, nonnative students often fail to realize that their English language skills may need improvement in the areas of writing, reading, listening comprehension, and speaking before they can succeed in various courses. If you are a nonnative student, take English as a second language (ESL) classes before tackling complex academic courses (see "A Note to Foreign Students and Nontraditional College Students" in this chapter).

Beware of taking too many courses that you think may be especially difficult for you in one semester. Spread these out over different semesters. If you work, keep your course load at a level you can handle comfortably in your nonworking hours. Although the figure will vary greatly depending on the requirements of a class (how much reading is expected, how many written assignments are due, how many tests there are, and your previous knowledge of and skills with the subject matter), most courses require about three hours of work outside class for every hour in class. Exhibit 2.1 shows how quickly the hours for schoolwork add up with an increased course load. For most people, taking a year longer to graduate or transfer would be better than earning a low grade point average (GPA). That low average may force you to repeat courses or take additional classes in order to try to raise your average before you can transfer.

If possible, take courses that you think may be interesting to you before you take less appealing required courses. Those less appealing topics may become more significant and enjoyable to you after you gain more knowledge and more experience as a student. Use your high school experience as a guide to determine which topics might interest you most and in which classes you might perform best. Your study habits and skills are not likely to take a large leap forward from June to September, so ask yourself, "What kind of student was I in high school? Was I able to handle several difficult courses at one time?" Let the answers to these types of questions guide you in your choices of the type and number of classes you take. As you develop better study skills, raise your self-confidence, and determine the educational direction you wish to take, you will be better equipped for more challenging classes.

Returning college students are often more motivated and goal oriented than students attending college directly out of high school. Some returning students may be more motivated to succeed because they are trying to improve their economic status through additional education as fast as possible. However, this more serious attitude often translates into anxiety about one's abilities. If you fall into this category, *take it easy*. Enroll in a light course load the first few semesters to give yourself time to get used to studying for examinations, writing class papers, and adjusting to the college environment. As your skills develop, so will your self-confidence. Although this approach may not seem practical to you because of your desire to gain employment or better employment as soon as possible, it might save you time and money in the long run. By initially not taking on more than you can handle, you might be more likely to stay in college and succeed in reaching your educational goal (see "A Note to Foreign Students and Nontraditional College Students").

What should you do when a class you signed up for is closed before you are accepted into it? You may be content to take it at some other time. However, if the class is the only one that your schedule will allow, or if it is a prerequisite for additional classes, you may not wish to give up so easily. Some students who are enrolled in the class may not show up, creating last-minute positions. Find out if there is an official waiting list. If there is none, in advance of the class, go to the instructor and see if he or she would be willing to add you to the class or at least put you on a waiting list. If you cannot contact the instructor personally, write a note expressing the reasons that you wish to take that particular class and email it to the instructor or leave the note in the instructor's mailbox. Show up the first day of class to see if you have been added, or if the instructor will be able to add you at that time. For additional help in choosing classes, see Humboldt State University's "How to Choose Classes & Prepare a Schedule" at http://studentaffairs.humboldt.edu/handbook/choose_prepare_schedule.php.

Dropping Classes

here are numerous reasons that you might wish to drop a class. For example, after going over the syllabus and attending the first meeting or two, you might find that the class is not what you expected, that you do not have the prerequisite background needed to succeed, or that the requirements of the class are too time-consuming considering your other responsibilities. Or, you might get a less than satisfactory grade on your first or first few assignments, leading you to think about your options.

At some colleges you must drop a class within the first week or so. At others, you can drop a class without a penalty grade well into the semester or quarter. In schools where you have the opportunity to take at least one test before the drop date, do not be too hasty in deciding to drop the class if you do not do well on the first test.

Analyze the reasons behind your less than satisfactory performance. Perhaps you simply misunderstood the direction for the test. Did you put enough time into studying for it? Did you use the resources available to you such as a study guide, online study aids, the instructor's office hours (to ask questions), or tutors? Can you earn a passable grade in the class if you change your approach and do well on the remaining tests and graded assignments? Make a realistic assessment of your potential to improve and earn a grade you would be satisfied with before deciding whether to drop the class or not.

Especially if you believe that you studied efficiently for the test and still received a lower than expected grade, the first step in assessing the problem is to see the instructor or, in some cases, the teaching assistant (TA). Ask the instructor or TA if you can go over the test with him or her. Try to get advice on studying for the next test. Every instructor has a different style, and this includes the manner in which he or she creates tests. Try to get on the instructor's "wavelength." That is, try to determine what types of things he or she emphasizes on a test. One criterion in deciding on whether to continue in a class or drop it might be whether the instructor was accessible to you and whether he or she was willing to be helpful.

The second step is to look into the study skills resources available to you. The class syllabus might list such resources. The preface to the textbook (and often the back cover) will list the in-book pedagogical (learning) aids and any online supplements that go along with the book. These aids can be very valuable, so explore their possibilities. The college will most likely have a study skills center. Visit this center and inquire about tutors (see "Using Study Skills Centers and Taking Study Skills Courses" in Chapter 3).

In some cases dropping a course might be advisable. However, if you can salvage your standing in the class you will avoid wasting the time you have already spent in that class. And although one or two "withdrew from class" notations on your transcript may have little or no effect on your ability to transfer to a different school or enter a graduate program, a large number of such "withdrawals" can create a picture of a person who does not follow through with commitments.

Make sure you know the deadlines for dropping a class. At many schools there are a series of dates. For instance, there might be a deadline for dropping the class and receiving a full refund of the money that you paid for the class or there might be a series of prorated refund amounts (different refunds depending on how long you stayed in the class). If you drop the class before a specific date, the record of your enrollment might be completely erased (your transcript may not show the withdrawal). And there will be a final date that you will be able to drop the class and not receive a letter grade. If you miss that date and just stop coming to class, you might receive an F. Most colleges and universities make it the responsibility of the student to drop a course or request an incomplete grade from the instructor.

An incomplete grade might be given to a student who has finished most of the work for a class but for reasons such as illness or personal emergency cannot finish the class when everyone else does. Usually you have to make special arrangements with the instructor to get an incomplete grade. Then you have to fulfill the conditions of those arrangements in a specified amount of time in order to get a letter grade.

Do not assume an instructor will drop you for lack of attendance or give you an incomplete grade. If you miss a drop date for a legitimate reason, a reason that absolutely prevented you from dropping the class on time, some colleges might let you petition to drop the class or to receive an incomplete grade.

Of course, the most effective way to avoid dropping a class is to not enroll in the first place in a course for which you do not have the prerequisite skills or knowledge to succeed. In other words, assess your ability to do well in a class before you enroll in it (review the sections "Setting Realistic Goals" and "Seeing a Counselor or an Advisor" in this chapter).

Choosing Instructors

Sometimes a personality match or clash between an instructor and a student will at least partially determine the value that a class will have for the student. Consequently, when more than one instructor teaches a class in which you are going to enroll, put some effort into finding out about those instructors. In some cases, especially in upper-division courses, unless you are willing to go to another school during a winter or summer session or find some other alternative way of taking the class, you might not have the luxury of choice.

If you are a serious student, you will avoid the "easiest" instructor, because instructors who are not demanding are most likely depriving their students of valuable skills and knowledge. Your ability to cope in upper-division and graduate classes will depend on the development of study skills and knowledge in beginning classes. An instructor who does not require you to develop those skills, and who provides you with little information, can jeopardize your college career. Also to be avoided are instructors who are unreasonable in their requirements for attaining a good grade in a course. Unfortunately, it is very difficult and a relative matter to judge what is "unreasonable." You will find that when you are looking back on your college career, some of the classes with the most demanding instructors were the most valuable to you.

Evaluating the ability of an instructor to teach is no easy task. You can ask college counselors and instructors whose classes you have already taken for advice. If they offer an opinion, that opinion might be based on what they think of the instructor on a personal level rather than how that instructor teaches. You can ask other students, but they, like you, are "beginners" in the academic world. However,

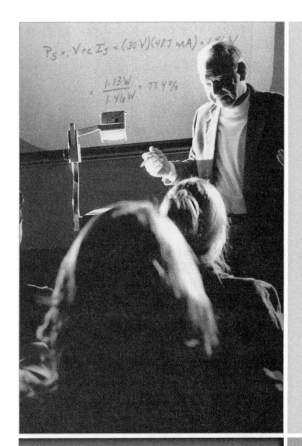

A good instructor will require you to develop skills to study, take notes, and do well on tests.

other students may provide you with a few insights if you ask them some of the following questions:

1. Did you learn very much from the instructor?
2. Was the instructor available to you during office hours?
3. Was the instructor reasonable in grading class material?
4. If you took an introductory course, did the instructor give you a good overview of the topics of the course to prepare you for more advanced courses in the subject?
5. Did the instructor emphasize only those things of interest to him or her, leaving out entire areas of the subject (as described in the catalog)?
6. Did the instructor present information in a well-organized and understandable manner?
7. Did the instructor seem to be up to date in relationship to the topics he or she lectured on in class? Did the instructor use old films and assign old reading material to the class?
8. Was the instructor enthusiastic about the subject he or she taught? Did you become more interested in the subject or the class as a result of the instructor's enthusiasm?
9. Did you enjoy or dread going to class, and why?
10. Would you recommend this instructor?

Of course, you must "consider the source." A serious and motivated student may evaluate an instructor far differently from a poor or uninterested student. Ask the people whom you are soliciting for advice what grade they received in the course. Give the reports of those who received As and Bs more weight than those of students who received Ds or Fs. If you can, go to a meeting of the honor society to ask honor students about instructors.

If you must take a course for which there is only one instructor and that instructor has a universally bad reputation, you may want to take the course at a different school. You may be able to do this during the summer.

If you are taking a course with multiple sections and instructors, find out about each of the instructors. Certainly never take a specific section just because it is at a good time. *It is much better to juggle your schedule as necessary to accommodate a good choice of classes and instructors.*

Some schools publish a book of student evaluations of instructors. At other schools, the student government offices might have records of teacher evaluations that students can review. This type of information is valuable as long as it is read critically. Additionally, prior to the semester that you plan to take a course, you may be able to "sit in" on one or more professors who teach the course. (Always request permission first.) Doing this for one or two sessions, especially in conjunction with other methods of evaluation, is an excellent aid to making choices of courses and instructors.

Some websites rate professors on the basis of student input. These sites may be specific to an individual school or national sites. Here are two national sites:

RateMyProfessors.com at www.ratemyprofessors.com/index.jsp

ProfessorPerformance.com at www.professorperformance.com/

One problem with these types of sites is that the students rating the professors are anonymous. You have no way of knowing whether they are conscientious students dedicated to learning or not. Some students who received a deserved bad grade might simply be seeking revenge by giving a bad rating to a professor. Conversely, students tend to give high ratings to professors who are less demanding, "friendly," or have a good sense of humor. A good sense of humor and being approachable are certainly positive characteristics. However, if you are serious about learning, such things as not requiring homework, not having to read the assigned books, having extremely easy tests, or giving a lot of extra credit are not necessarily the characteristics that you should be looking for when choosing an instructor.

It is much better to ask students in person about what they think of a professor and evaluate their opinions on the basis of what you know about those students. When you do this, you can also follow up one question with another to better determine the basis of an opinion. However, I include information on these sites because thousands of students consult them every day. If you do consult an Internet site that rates professors, pay attention only to average ratings and then only when a large number of students have rated the professor. Even with a relatively large number of ratings, say more than 100, the average rating is not based on a random representative sample, so be skeptical. In addition, the sites have no way of controlling or knowing who is doing the rating. The instructor could rate himself or herself. A particular group of students who, for some reason, especially liked or disliked the professor might rate that professor and skew the resulting average. Read students' comments on the professor in question to determine whether there is any consensus about his or her teaching characteristics. If the information is available, check to see if all of the comments were posted in one semester or over a broad period of time. Those posted over a span of time, if consistent, might have a greater element of reliability than if all of the opinions were posted at the same time. This is because a large number of postings at the same time might have been done by a particular group of students with a specific agenda (or even the same student rating several times), making the ratings even less representative than other professors' ratings that were posted over many semesters or quarters. In all cases, be cautious about the information you gather from these sites.

Alternatives to the Usual Way of Getting Credit

The usual way to get unit credit in a college or university is to attend regular lectures for courses (or participate in lab classes) listed in the catalog and successfully complete the requirements for those courses. The number of units granted for undergraduate courses is most often dependent on how many hours of lecture there are for a course in a term.

There are many other ways to get college or university credit. Not all institutions allow all of the common alternative methods listed next, so check your college's catalog. Also check to see how many units can be granted for each method.

1. Credit by Examination

There are several possible ways to get college credit by taking examinations. Some of these examinations test your proficiency in a particular class or course of study that you completed in high school. Colleges also may allow credit for subjects for which you did not take formal classes but for which you can demonstrate proficiency at a certain level. Specifics for these possibilities are as follows:

■ **High school students can get college credit by taking advanced placement examinations.** If you are still in high school, see your counselor for information on this program. You can also consult The College Board's "About AP" at www.collegeboard.com/student/testing/ap/about.html.

■ **Some institutions give English equivalency examinations.** A student usually can gain three to six units of credit by passing such exams.

Many colleges use a standardized test in the College-Level Examination Program (CLEP) to test English competency.

■ **Explore numerous other CLEP tests.** These tests are available for mathematics, humanities, natural science, social science, history, general science, business, composition and literature, and foreign language. See your college's catalog for specifics on which tests (if any) you can take and how many units you may accumulate by passing CLEP tests. If you decide to take a CLEP test, you may wish to consult the most recent edition of one of the many books that give advice on how to pass these tests along with sample questions. (See "About CLEP: Shorten Your Path to a College Degree—With CLEP!" at www.collegeboard.com/student/testing/clep/about.html.)

■ **Any department on campus may allow students to demonstrate competence in a course by successfully passing a standardized test.** At one California university, students are allowed to get advanced placement credit and up to 30 semester units applied to a baccalaureate degree based on other types of credit by examination. If you decide to use this option, talk to the person responsible for administering any test you will take. Find out if there are back tests that you can look at, what books you should read, and what other preparation should be done to complete the test successfully.

2. Online (Web-Based) Courses

Students can do all or some of their coursework for a bachelor's degree, some graduate degrees, continuing education requirements, and some vocational degrees and certificates online. Online work and other types of educational programs that are accomplished or predominately done off campus are generally referred to as distance education. Most colleges and universities offer their own online courses. These courses can be used to receive credit along with traditional on-campus classes. Some online classes require that you attend classroom meetings as well, and others are done exclusively online. Some online courses allow you to proceed at your own pace, whereas others require you to be online at specific times of the day and have very specific deadlines for assignments.

If your college does not offer a course that you might like to take online, other colleges might. Check with your college counselor to see if you can take online courses from other institutions and if there is a limit on how many you can take. If you intend to work toward a degree totally online, make sure that the institution offering the degree is fully accredited and that the degree will be accepted as such by potential employers and other educational institutions. It is worthwhile to investigate the online institution you might attend; otherwise, you could lose thousands of dollars and a lot of time. (See www.world-wide learn.com for a catalog of institutions that offer online degrees and certificates or individual courses.)

Online courses offer several advantages. They often allow flexibility in scheduling and allow you to schedule other activities (such as work) around your classes. You can work from your home (or any place there is an Internet connection) and save money on transportation, food, and child-care costs. However, there are also disadvantages to online classes. They might actually require more of your time than on-campus classes. They require you to read a lot of material online, communicate with the professor online, and often communicate online with other students taking the course. You must be a self-motivated person who does not procrastinate in order to succeed when taking an online course. For some other pitfalls of online classes, see *Ten Disadvantages of Online Courses* at www.montgomerycollege.edu/Departments/studevgt/onlinsts/disad.htm. For advantages of online classes and other information about them, see the United States Distance Learning Association's site at www.usdla.org.

3. Instructional Television

Some institutions produce or subscribe to educational programs that are shown on television. The variety of courses is usually very limited, but it is a way to get some units in a nontraditional manner. The advantages and disadvantages of instructional television are similar to those of taking online classes.

4. Cooperative Education

Cooperative education programs are a way to get college credit for paid or voluntary work. They may involve some classroom time, often with guest speakers. But basically you are getting credit for working, reporting on your work, and being evaluated by your employer. Cooperative education is designed to teach you how to market yourself, enhance your self-esteem, handle communication problems, and make career decisions. See the National Commission for Cooperative Education's website at www.co-op.edu/.

5. Directed or Independent Study

Many schools allow students to gain some credits for projects that they do on their own. Usually each academic department determines the requirements for such credit. Typically, a student meets with a specific instructor, often one whom the student has had for a traditional course, and arranges to do the independent study. Usually there are prerequisites to being accepted into such a program. For instance, you may have to have a specific number of units for courses in a specific department to do an independent study in that department.

6. Extension Courses

Some schools will allow a certain amount of credit to be gained by taking courses through college extension programs. Extension programs are sometimes called community education, because they are courses offered to the general public by a college or university. Extension programs often include noncredit courses in a wide variety of fields as well as classes for children and seniors.

A person does not have to be accepted for admission to the college or university in order to take an extension course. However, a person who is a regularly enrolled student can also take extension courses. The extension program will have its own catalog of courses, and usually this catalog will indicate which courses are available for regular college credit. Often the student has to submit proof that these courses were equivalent in their academic standards to regular college courses. This is especially true if you take an extension class at a college or university in which you are not enrolled. It is much more likely that you will find extension classes offered for college credit at a four-year school than at a community college. Many major universities have large extension programs. For an example of an extension program at a major university, see www.uclaextension.edu/.

7. Life Experience

Some schools allow credit for learning, knowledge, or skills based on non-collegiate activities; in other words, they may give credit for experiences gained from jobs or other life experience and activities. Schools that grant such credit establish their own criteria for awarding the credit. Whether prior experience is worthy of college credit might be based on an examination (see "1. Credit by Examination"). Or, some colleges might give credit for paid or nonpaid internships or for the presentation of a portfolio. Some types of volunteer work may qualify for unit credit. Another type of life experience that might provide college credit is military service (see below).

8. Non–Collegiate-Sponsored Training Programs

Some colleges and universities give college credit for various types of training programs, including those offered by the military. If you have ever been enrolled in a training program, consult your college counselor to determine whether it qualifies for college credit.

9. Credit for Military Service

One specific type of life experience credit you could be eligible to receive is for military service. Some colleges give elective unit credit for just having been in the military for a specific amount of time. You may also receive credit for educational and training courses completed in the military if those courses meet certain standards. See a counselor for the details on how to apply for this credit. To learn more about getting credit for military service, see "College Credit for Military Service" at www.military.com/ Content/MoreContent1/?file=college_credit.

Credit/No Credit Option

Most colleges and universities allow students to take a certain amount of units as credit/no credit (pass/fail) courses. That is, at the end of a term, if a student has achieved a certain grade (often a C), that student will get credit for the course. If the student gets a lower grade than required, the student does not receive any credit for the course. In either case, at most schools, the credit/no credit grade does not affect the student's GPA.

One of the rationales for the credit/no credit option is that it allows students to explore courses in fields in which they might be interested but in which they lack academic experience. Allowing a student to take a course as credit/no credit might encourage exploration without the anxiety that might be attached to working for a high grade in an uncharted field. The credit/no credit option might also reduce the stress of taking a course in a field in which a student knows from previous experience that he or she is not very adept. Another advantage of this option is that the student can deemphasize a course that he or she is taking for credit/no credit and, therefore, devote more time to other courses that are more important for the student's major.

A potential disadvantage of the credit/no credit option is that if a course is deemphasized to the point that the student does not pass it, whatever time the student put into the course will have been wasted. An opposite type of situation can also occur. The student may have gotten an A or a B in the course if the credit/no credit option had not been used. That A or B could have been valuable in raising or maintaining a GPA. A student usually has to choose between a letter grade and credit/no credit early in a term. *Once the decision is made most schools will not allow it to be changed.*

If a course is in your major or a requirement for your major, do not take it as credit/no credit. Most colleges do not count the units gained by simply getting credit for them toward a student's requirements for his or her major. Even if the school you are currently attending will accept a limited number of pass or credit grades, if you transfer to a different school, or go to graduate school, the new school may not accept the units for such a course, because a B or better in these courses may be required. Because there will be no record of an actual grade on your transcript, you may be required to repeat the course.

As you can see, the consequences of using the credit/no credit option can be serious. Before taking a course as credit/no credit, seek the advice of a counselor or consult with the instructor.

Auditing Classes

To audit a class means to sit in on it without taking it for a grade or for any type of credit. At most colleges you have to pay an auditing fee. A person who is interested in a subject, but does not want the stress of doing assigned homework or studying for tests, might audit a course on a topic of interest. Such a person might not be working on completing the requirements for a degree, so credit for the course might be seen as unimportant. Others may think about auditing a class because they do not have the confidence to take the class for credit the first time around. However, auditing a class before taking it for credit is obviously time-consuming. And, even if you come to believe that you could do well in a class, most colleges will not allow you to change your enrollment status so that you can receive credit. Rather than audit a class, see if there is a lower-level course in the area that you were going to audit. You could take that class *for credit* and it might prepare you for the course you were thinking about auditing. In any case, always discuss the benefits and liabilities of auditing a class with the instructor who is teaching the class and/or a counselor.

Seeing a Counselor or an Advisor

There are usually many different types of counselors or advisors at a college. Academic counselors act as a link between students and the faculty and administration. They guide students toward their academic goals in terms of choosing their curriculum, degree, and major, as well as their career. Academic counselors often handle orientation sessions and inform students about their college's resources and policies.

If you are interested in a course but do not want the added stress of doing homework and taking tests, you may choose to audit the course.

Academic counselors can save you a lot of "wheel spinning." If you are attending a two-year school and plan to transfer, a counselor can assist you in determining transfer requirements. It is also a good idea to talk to counselors at the school to which you plan to transfer. They may be aware of recent changes in requirements that your counselor is not. In general, academic counselors or advisors can guide you through what often appears to be a confusing maze of graduation requirements.

Individual departments often have their own advisors. If you are interested in a specific major, talk to the advisor in that department both at your current school and at the school to which you plan to transfer; between them, they often can direct you specifically toward your goals. It is also valuable to talk to a recent graduate of the program in which you are interested in entering.

In addition to educational planning, the counseling department can often help in personal (crisis) counseling. Such personal counseling (make sure that you are seeing a *licensed* therapist) can make the difference between a student reaching his or her educational goal or dropping out of college. Sometimes loneliness due to separation from family and friends, or difficulty adjusting to life away from home, can seem overwhelming. Personal counseling sessions and college-sponsored workshops on crisis management can help students cope with these problems, and other problems as well. College counseling departments may offer counseling for alcohol and drug abuse, eating disorders, dealing with rape, family intervention, stress reduction, depression, thoughts of suicide, problems of gender identity, and stresses of the working student. Just as it is wise to seek medical help for physical problems, it is a wise and often a life-changing and sometimes a life-saving decision to seek personal counseling when needed.

Most schools provide veterans' counseling, career planning, financial aid, and legal advice referrals as well. Colleges also have special counselors for disabled students and special services for such students. See "A Note to Students with Disabilities" in this chapter.

The Consequences of Low Grades

The importance of grades once you have left school is debatable, although competition for some jobs may be resolved partially on the basis of grades earned in college. Despite one U.S. president's recent bragging about his C average, the public does not usually know how well a politician performed in college. Most people do not inquire into the class ranking of their doctors, dentists, lawyers, or pharmacists, or know how well their auto mechanics, plumbers, or electricians performed in vocational school. If we generally do not judge people by grades after they graduate, why all the fuss about grades?

The main consequence of grades is how they affect a student's life in school. Various minimal GPAs are needed in order to take certain courses; transfer from a community college to a four-year school; get into a graduate or professional school; be eligible for athletics; join certain clubs or groups; get scholarships, fellowships, or grants; run for school offices; and simply stay in school. For these reasons, students should strive to maintain a good GPA.

Even a few Ds or Fs can be devastating to a GPA. For instance, if you have three classes (three semester units each) and receive a B, a C, and an F, your GPA will be 1.67 (based on a system in which an A = 4 and an F = 0 grade points). By contrast, if you receive a B, a C, and a C, your GPA will be 2.34. The 1.67 could put you on academic probation. Academic probation is a warning to students that their academic performance is not satisfactory and that if they do not improve that performance they will be dismissed from college. To stay off academic probation, a student must improve his or her GPA in a specific amount of time to a level determined by the college. The exact conditions on which a student would be placed on academic probation and the conditions to be removed from probation will vary. However, many schools that use a grade point system in which 4 is the highest grade place students on academic probation if their GPA drops below 2.0. Your college catalog will explain your school's policy on this. Exhibit 2.6 shows three other possible grade summaries for a semester or quarter.

Remember, an F and an A average out to a C. The more Ds and Fs you accumulate, the longer it will take for you to reach a GPA that will allow you to advance academically.

In addition to their effect on GPAs, low course grades can be devastating to one's self-confidence and self-esteem. And low grades are unnecessary. As cautioned earlier in this guide, do not attempt to take courses you do not have the skills to complete. If this is not obvious beforehand, it soon will be. It might be better to drop a course, if possible, after getting poor test scores or other poor grades and "write off" that investment of time than to wind up with a low grade. However, do not take dropping a class lightly. Analyze the possibility that with increased effort or help you could receive a passable grade in the class and perhaps discuss that possibility with the instructor (see "Dropping Classes" in this chapter).

Getting the Most Out of College Life

A college is an institution, but it should not make you feel "institutionalized." Rather, it should encourage a flowering of your individuality. However, people who do not do well in school are bound to feel constrained by school, causing them to dislike the college experience. This book provides some guidelines (and references to sources of other guidelines) that may help you improve your performance and thus your enjoyment of college. A poor or even mediocre performance will cause frustration and make your college experience unrewarding.

Another reason some students dislike college is that they suffer from a feeling of alienation. They are lost in what often seems an impersonal world. Here are some suggestions to turn this feeling into one of belonging:

1. **Make an active effort to meet other students.** Even before the first day of school you can often meet students on the Internet. One popular resource to do this is called FaceBook. It is an Internet social resource that allows you to see student profiles and photographs of students at your university and other universities in its database. It allows you to see what classes other students are taking, and to find people with common academic and

EXHIBIT 2.6   The effect of low grades on grade-point average (GPA).

In this example, an A = 4; a B = 3; a C = 2; a D = 1; and an F = 0 grade points.

NAME OF COURSE	UNITS	GRADE	GRADE POINTS
SITUATION #1			
Sociology 1	3	C	6
Mathematics 12	3	C	6
Humanities 1	3	D	3
Philosophy 6	3	F	0
History 2	3	C	6
Total grade points			21
GPA			1.4 (21/15)
SITUATION #2			
Sociology 1	3	C	6
Mathematics 12	3	B	9
Humanities 1	3	B	9
Philosophy 6	3	C	6
History 2	3	C	6
Total grade points			39
GPA			2.6 (39/15)
SITUATION #3			
Sociology 1	3	B	9
Mathematics 12	3	B	9
Humanities 1	3	B	9
Philosophy 6	3	A	12
History 2	3	A	12
Total grade points			51
GPA			3.4 (51/15)

nonacademic interests. The service is available at hundreds of schools and is free. To make use of the service you have to be registered on the network and provide an email address. You can then upload your picture or pictures and personal information to the network. Some students use this to establish a social footing before the first day of their first semester, and they then use the system to expand that network as they progress through the years at the college. You can advertise parties, contact people in your classes, find out about and join FaceBook groups and clubs, and so on. There are, however, downsides to FaceBook. Some students become "addicted" to this site, and other such sites. Some students even compete to see how many online friends they can make. This takes time away from other activities such as schoolwork and face-to-face relationships. Of course, if you value total privacy, this system would not be for you; at the least, limit the amount and type of information that you supply. There is also the chance that you might receive attention from people with whom you do not wish to associate, so take that into consideration before you register. If you are interested in this service, you can find it at www.facebook.com/. For information on potential problems with such sites, including identity theft and stalking, see www.sonoma.edu/star/issue6/the_facebook.html.

You can also meet people the old-fashioned way. At college orientations or on the first day of classes, talk to a lot of other students. If you find students who seem to be compatible with you, get their contact information. Even if your attempts do not work out the first time around, continue to try to meet people that might help you feel less isolated. This is especially important if you are attending school away from home, where you have an established network of family and friends.

2. **Get involved in school clubs or organizations.** The school catalog might list these, or you can get a list from the office of the Dean of Student Services. However, be careful not to become so involved in extracurricular activities that those activities distract from your educational goals.

3. **Think about running for a student body office or volunteering to be on a student body committee.** Being involved in student government puts you in a position to share in making important decisions that impact students. At many schools that have a policy of shared governance, students play an important role. Of course, being involved in student government provides experience for students planning to go into fields such as political science, law, and business. It is also a good way to meet people.

4. **Contribute to the school newspaper.** You may have to be enrolled in a journalism class to do this. However, many schools allow students who

are not enrolled to contribute to the newspaper in a variety of ways such as writing a special feature article or doing political cartooning.

5. **If you must work, attempt to get a job on campus.** In addition to jobs in shops and offices on campus, there may be jobs as TAs, research assistants, instructional assistants, and resident advisors. Some of these jobs may not be available to new students.

Many campus jobs can provide you with a great opportunity to interact with other students and often faculty. Working on campus also cuts down on travel time and gives you a feeling of being a valuable part of the college. In addition, depending on the job, working on campus might be more useful to you in the future than working off campus. For instance, if you work for an academic department and you plan to go to graduate school, your supervisor could write a letter of recommendation for you. Of course, if you work in an off-campus job that is related to your field of study, you may receive the same benefit.

6. **Attend school athletic and other events.** This can give you a feeling of being part of the school community and culture. It can also be fun.

7. **Attend school plays, concerts, dances, and special lectures.** These activities are fun ways to get acquainted with other students.

8. **Meet your instructors.** Even if you are doing well in your classes, visit each instructor in his or her office at least once during the semester to discuss the class. At some point, you might wish to ask some of your instructors for academic references, and making "personal" contacts with your instructors will likely benefit you in this regard.

9. **Study in groups (when appropriate).** This is a way to make friends and develop a feeling of teamwork. For more on this topic, see "Critical Thinking" in Chapter 3.

10. **Visit areas of the campus that you have not seen.** For instance, even if you are not an art student, go to the art department to look at displays or the art museum, if one exists. Other possible areas you can visit are botanical gardens, student lounges, and special libraries.

College Life Is Not for Everyone

Although the aim of this book is to help students succeed in college, it is important to realize that college is not for everyone. At least, at certain times in one's life, college might not be the correct path to pursue.

We live in a culture that emphasizes degrees. Today, because of the extreme emphasis on the importance of a college education, increasing numbers of people living in the United States are attending college. However, just like active participation in competitive athletics might not work for everyone, university-type academic training might not be for everyone. Vocational schools or simply entering the job market might be better matches to some peoples' personalities, skills, and ambitions.

People should not put themselves in situations in which they always fail or are unhappy. If you do not feel that you are prepared for college, or if you have no interest in it, you might wish to consider some alternative choices. If you have tried your hardest to succeed in college and have failed, or if you simply do not enjoy the college environment, perhaps you should direct your energies in another direction. As I have said, college is not for everyone, nor is it for everyone at the same chronological time. Many 17- and 18-year-olds take to college life immediately, but others do better if they go to college 2, 5, 10, or more years after high school. The decision to go to college is a commitment that may be too overwhelming for certain people at certain points in their lives. Try to analyze your current needs or go to a vocational counselor for help in doing so. He or she may suggest various academic assessment tests as well as tests for vocational interests. Use these tests as one resource in making your decision to attend or not to attend college.

Pitfalls of College Life and Campus Crime

Some of the pitfalls of college are emotional challenges, alcohol and drug abuse, and crime. Every student needs to be aware of these potential problems.

Emotional Challenges

The pressures of college life can lead to depression, frustration, and anxiety. About 30 percent of college freshmen report feeling overwhelmed by college life. Of course, not everyone who is initially besieged by changes in their life is or will become clinically depressed. A person is considered to be suffering from depression when he or she has feelings of sadness or of unbearable stress for weeks or longer.

There are many causes of depression, frustration, and anxiety. However, one cause of these emotional problems is not living up to one's own expectations for one's self or the expectations of others. Depression and lesser emotional problems might also result simply from the large number of adjustments you will have to make by attending college for the first time, especially if you are going to be living away from home. You might be separated from family, friends, and your familiar routine. You might be having troubles forming new relationships, both platonic (friendly) and romantic. You might have financial worries and concerns about what happens after college. You might have to fend for yourself for the first time. The National Mental Health Association suggests that students who experience prolonged sadness or feel under extreme stress should do the following:

1. *Carefully plan each day and prioritize your daily, weekly, and monthly activities.* (See "Time Management" in Chapter 3.)
2. *Get the amount of sleep you need to feel well.* For most people that is seven or eight hours a night. Constant fatigue is a major contributor to depression.
3. *Participate in college activities.* (See "Getting the Most Out of College Life" in this chapter.)
4. *Actively seek support from family and friends.*
5. *Try relaxation methods.* (See "Stress Management" in Chapter 3.)
6. *Take some time each day to do something that you really want to do.* This will give you a feeling of control over your life.
7. *Last but certainly not least, seek medical treatment and professional counseling.* Often this is available on campus. Treatment might include psychological counseling and/or medication.

For a more detailed discussion of this information, see The National Mental Health Association's "Tips on Dealing with Depression in College" at www.nmha.org/infoctr/factsheets/DepressioninCollege.cfm.

For a comprehensive discussion of the types of depression, causes of depression, treatments for depression, suggestions on where to get help and how to help oneself, see the National Institute of Mental Health's online (and printable) booklet called *Depression* at www.nimh.nih.gov/publicat/depression.cfm. Also see Brigham and Women's Hospital's "Depression in College" at http://healthgate.partners.org/browsing/browseContent.asp?fileName=47093. xml&title=Depression%20In%20College.

Alcohol and Drug Abuse

Another pitfall of college life is the temptation to drink too much alcohol and take dangerous drugs. In 2002, about 1,400 students between the ages of 18 and 24 died of alcohol-related injuries and about 31 percent of students abused alcohol; about 500,000 students were injured while under the influence of alcohol; 600,000 students were assaulted by other students who had been drinking; more than 70,000 students were the victims of alcohol-related sexual assault or date rape; hundreds of thousands of students had unprotected sex, and many reported that they were too intoxicated to even know if they had had sex; about 25 percent of students reported that alcohol negatively influenced their academic success; 150,000 students developed alcohol-related health problems; and between 1.2 and 1.5 percent of students said they had attempted suicide within the last year because of alcohol or drug abuse. (See The National Institute on Alcohol Abuse and Alcoholism's website for the sources of these statistics and other relevant information. at www.collegedrinkingprevention.gov/facts/.)

In addition, alcohol intoxication is a contributor to about 2 million traffic accidents involving students. It is also a factor in many other behaviors that adversely affect school life and can bring students into negative contact with the police.

Excessive drinking might negatively affect not only the student, but the student's family, friends, and the community (through acts of public drunkenness, car accidents, assaults, and property damage). The statistics on alcohol abuse were given to show that this type of abuse is a massive problem on college campuses. I am not going to go into the statistics of nonalcoholic drugs on campus, but abuse of both illegal and legal drugs is also a big problem. Drug abuse creates similar problems to those caused by alcohol abuse. If you have any type of alcohol or other drug problem, consult a crisis counselor or a drug abuse counselor. Many schools offer this service free of charge. You can also consult the following websites:

> The National Institute on Alcohol Abuse and Alcoholism site (URL given above) gives advice on how to cut down on drinking.

> Facts on Tap at www.factsontap.org/. This site is dedicated to the prevention and intervention of alcohol and drug problems experienced by college students.

Campus Crime

Another situation that one might face on campus is crime. Anyone can be a victim of crime. Unfortunately, college campuses are not safe havens. Although most college campuses are in general safer than many other places, crimes of all types occur on college campuses and in the neighborhoods surrounding them. Students should be aware of the crime statistics for their campus and surrounding areas.

The Jeanne Clery Disclosure of Campus Security Policy and Campus Crime Statistics Act is a federal law that requires colleges and universities to report crimes that occurred on their campuses. The U. S. Department of Education collects and distributes information on crime. You should be able to get the crime statistics for your campus from the campus police. You can also find out more about the Clery Act, related laws, and crime statistics at the website Security on Campus at www.securityoncampus.org/. In addition, this website has links to recent articles on campus crime, a section on victims rights, and numerous other features.

The federal Office of Victims of Crime (OVC) also has important information on all aspects of campus crime, including victim assistance and compensation programs. It can be found at www.ojp.usdoj.gov/ovc/help/cc.htm.

Obtaining Financial Support

Parents and jobs are two common sources of financial support for a college education. If parental support is insufficient or unavailable, however, the second can pose problems. Working many hours a week can detract from a student's schoolwork.

You must balance immediate financial needs with ultimate goals. For most people, working 40 hours or more a week is probably not compatible with taking 15 or more semester units (see Exhibit 2.7). A low GPA and

EXHIBIT 2.7 Number of hours of work and suggested number of units to take in college.*

NUMBER OF WORK HOURS	NUMBER OF SCHOOL UNITS
40	6
30	9
20	12
5 or less	12-15

*This is meant to be a rough guideline. Each individual's motivation and energy level, personal circumstances (health, family obligations, etc.), and academic and organizational skills, will influence the relationship between the number of work hours and success in college. Try to be realistic in assessing your own limitations.

fatigue are probable outcomes. You may be able to lessen your job workload by applying for one or more of the following:

1. federal grants and loans
2. federal work-study programs
3. state grants and loans
4. scholarships
5. local monies for students

About 70 percent of all of the financial aid to college students in the United States comes from the U.S. Department of Education's Federal Student Aid (FSA) programs. Many people do not apply for financial aid because of misconceptions about how it is appropriated. Federal financial aid is not based on ethnicity or race and you do not have to be impoverished to receive it. So, the first step to receiving federal financial aid is for you to learn the government's programs.

All students who plan to attend college should file a Free Application for Federal Student Aid (FAFSA) each year. Check the FAFSA website at www.fafsa.ed.gov/ for deadlines. You may need to file a FAFSA to apply for financial aid from sources other than the federal government such as from your state or your university. The deadlines for these sources of money may be different from the FAFSA filing date. Many colleges require students to file for state grants when they file for any financial aid at the school (discussed later).

A student may wish to go to an expensive college but think that he or she cannot afford it. However, this is not necessarily the case. For each college to which a student applies, the student should send a copy of his or her FAFSA. Each college will then determine how much the student will have to pay and what combination of loans, grants, and scholarships it can offer that student. When a student is unsure of where to attend college, a good financial offer from a college can make the difference.

The federal government provides some grants. Grants do not have to be paid back. Two types of need-based grants are Federal Pell Grants and Federal Supplemental Educational Opportunity Grants.

The federal government also provides loans. Loans are monies that have to be paid back. Federal loans generally carry lower interest rates than private loans and usually do not have to be paid back until you finish school. The amount of money that the government will loan you depends on how many years you have been in college and whether you are financially dependent on your parents or whether you support yourself.

The Federal Work-Study Program (FWSP) subsidizes the salaries paid to students during the summer and also times of enrollment. Work study can be on campus or off, and it can be with nonprofit or for-profit employers. Work study provides the student with funds and also work experience. Get up-to-date details on this program from your college's financial aid office. Also see the FWSP's website at www.ed.gov/prog_info/SFA/StudentGuide/2002–3/workstudy.html.

The Department of Education has a website that provides detailed sections on filling out the free application for student aid at www.fafsa.ed.gov/. This site has all the information that you need to fill out the necessary form, and you can print the form from the site or obtain it from your school's financial aid office.

In addition to the federal government, state agencies, private foundations, and individuals make monies available to students in need of financial aid. There are literally thousands of sources for, and types of, grants, loans, scholarships, and employment opportunities. Your college catalog or your college's financial aid office will have details on how to apply.

Very often high school and college students get letters from companies offering to find scholarships for students for a fee. Be skeptical of these companies. College financial aid offices and high school counselors can often offer the same lists of scholarships for free. Students can also get scholarship information for free from numerous scholarship websites. Here are some of these sites:

FastWeb at http://fastweb.monster.com/

Mach 25 at www.collegenet.com/mach25/

Fast Aid at www.fastaid.com/

The Scholarship Page! at www.scholarship-page.com/

College Answer at www.collegeanswer.com/index.jsp

Scholarship Resource Network Express at www.srnexpress.com/index.cfm

Remember, when you reach your educational goal (bachelor's, master's, or doctor's degree or certificate), your earning power will most likely be greater than it currently is (see Exhibit 2.8). Delaying that ultimate goal in order to work more than the hours necessary for your general support may be counterproductive. Of course, that is a matter of personal choice and philosophy.

You might try to obtain employment in an area related to your major. Some colleges even offer credit for such employment. See a counselor for information about this. In addition, in a competitive job market, a new

| EXHIBIT 2.8 | Economic returns of additional education. |

EDUCATIONAL ATTAINMENT	MEAN EARNINGS BY HIGHEST DEGREE EARNED: 2003
Not a High School Graduate	$18,734
High School Graduate	$27,915
Some College (no degree)	$29,533
Associate Degree	$35,958
Bachelor's Degree	$51,206
Master's Degree	$62,514
Doctorate Degree	$88,471

From the U.S. Bureau of the Census, Table 9: Earnings in 2003 by Educational Attainment of Worker 18 Years and Over. This study was released in March 2005. The complete report can be found at www.census.gov/population/socdemo/education/cps2004/tab09-1.pdf

graduate who has experience in a field may have an advantage over applicants without experience.

One way to attain experience is through internships. Internships can be paid or unpaid. However, even an unpaid internship can give you future opportunity dividends. The job experience you receive during an internship looks good on a resume. You might gain full-time employment after you graduate from the place where you did your internship, or you might get good letters of recommendation from your internship supervisor. For more information on internships, see "Alternatives to the Usual Way of Getting Credit" in this chapter and "Career Planning and Getting a Job" in Chapter 4.

Information on union-sponsored scholarships can be obtained by writing to AFL-CIO, 815 16th Street NW, Washington, DC 20006.

Also visit these websites:

The Student Guide:
http://studentaid.ed.gov/students/publications/student_guide/2004_2005/english/types-stafford.htm

FinAid! at www.finaid.org/

EdFund at www.edwise.org/

The First Day of Class

The first day of class sets the scene for the entire semester or quarter. Although some professors may simply take roll, pass out a syllabus, and dismiss the class, believing in the notion that "nothing happens" on the first day is detrimental to your success. At this time, you usually find out details about the subject matter of the course. You also learn what knowledge and skills the instructor assumes you already have, and what will be required of you on tests, term papers, and other assignments. Failure to understand these requirements may result in less than satisfactory results in the class. You also have the opportunity on the first day to ask the instructor questions if any of the class requirements seem vague to you.

If you miss the first day of class, make sure you get all of the information that was presented, including any printed material that was handed out. Read the course syllabus or outline carefully; make sure you understand all the items explained in the printed material. Keep all printed material until the end of the term and refer to it as necessary. Be warned, however, that the instructor might have made last-minute changes and additions to such printed material—another reason your presence on the first day is important. In addition, the "tone" of the class is set the first day, and this might not be apparent by simply reading the syllabus.

Based on the "tone" and requirements of the class, a student may choose to drop the class for a variety of reasons. If you make this determination on the first day, there may be time to find another class.

Instructors often deviate from the official college suggestions for certain requirements. For instance, some instructors drop students after three absences regardless of the students' performance. Other instructors never drop students for lack of attendance. Some instructors do not give makeup exams; others do. Those who do may have all kinds of different policies for making up tests. Make sure you understand these and any other policies specific to each class you take.

It is also a good idea to buy (or review) your textbook early. Read the preface, introduction, and each chapter's summary. This should give you an idea of the tone and coverage of the class. Also, familiarize yourself with any learning aids the book offers (online learning centers, research tools, study guides, glossaries, and so on).

Still another reason for attending the first day of class is that some professors drop those who do not attend and add students on waiting lists in their place. It is particularly important to attend the first day of class if you are on a waiting list or are "running for class." "Running for class" means attending a class that is closed with the hope that openings may occur. If you cannot attend the first day, inform the professor beforehand. But be cautioned: some instructors may not accept written excuses.

Getting in Touch with a Professor

Most schools will have an online directory of the entire faculty. The directory might list the location of each instructor's office, his or her telephone number, and an email address. Of course, this information can also be obtained from a school's information desk or Office of Academic Affairs.

The faculty directory might also provide a link to the instructor's web page or you might be able to find an instructor's web page through a search engine. The professor's web page might provide important information about the course you are taking, links to other useful web pages, general information about the academic discipline of the professor, and personal information about the professor.

Student to Instructor Etiquette

Although most college instructors strive to be objective when assigning grades, human nature being what it is, an instructor's reaction to a student's behavior may influence his or her decision making. Just as your opinion of an instructor may influence your attitude toward the subject taught, the instructor's opinion of you may help shape (perhaps subtly) his or her evaluation of your performance in the class. And different instructors invite different types of behavior from their students. Some enjoy a rather free discussion of topics, enforcing minimal rules for turn taking. Others allow no time for discussion of the subject matter during a lecture period. It is wise to avoid agitating an instructor by learning what rules of participation are desired and adhering to them.

Remember that instructors, not surprisingly, believe their subject areas are important, so do not insult them with comments such as, "This is not my major, so I didn't study too much for the test." If you are to be thought of as a serious student, you must attempt to do your best for each subject you take. A comment professors often hear from past students is, "I didn't realize how much your course would help me in other classes," or "Your class has really helped me to understand political science" (or economics or race relations or some other course topic). The importance of some courses simply does not become apparent until some time after students have taken them. Students who fail to apply themselves in courses deemed unimportant are missing one of the main values and purposes of a liberal arts education (see "Why Do I Have to Take This Course? The Goals of Liberal Studies" in this chapter).

Other behaviors expected (or not expected) in college classes are as follows:

1. **Concentrate on the classroom activities during class time.** College instructors may be less tolerant of out-of-order talking or other rude behavior than high school teachers, who are usually more accustomed to disciplinary problems. College professors do not see themselves as baby-sitters but, rather, as adults teaching adults. Many become enormously agitated at interferences such as private discussions between students during a lecture. Most instructors do not consider class time to be social or even study time. It is a time to glean valuable knowledge from the instructor.

2. **Be on time and be prepared for note taking and tests (have the necessary equipment).** Tardiness is disruptive both to the instructor and to the students, and an instructor might feel no obligation to help you obtain any materials you should have known you would need.

3. **Stay for the complete class.** Leaving a class early can be even more disruptive than tardiness. If you need to leave a class early, inform the instructor of your plans to do so before class starts.

4. **Concentrate on the class.** While you are in class, do not read newspapers, study for tests, or do homework. Certainly, do not sleep! All such behaviors are insulting to an instructor.

5. **Turn off cell phones.** Phones ringing or musical tones going off in class are disruptive and will be considered inconsiderate behavior on your part.

6. **If you miss a class, refrain from asking your instructor, "Did I miss anything important?"** Many instructors would like a license to kill over this one. *Of course, you missed something important* (unless the instructor was also absent and class was not held).

7. **If you miss a class, catch up.** Borrow someone's notes and photocopy them. Then ask the instructor or other students to clarify anything you do not understand in the notes. You could also visit the

instructor during office hours or email him or her with questions about the material you missed.

8. **Do not call an instructor by his or her first name unless invited to do so.** Some instructors are very informal, but others may be offended by an informal address. Using "Professor" and the instructor's last name is always acceptable.

9. **Follow the instructor's lead regarding interaction.** Some professors do not mind talking to students about matters not related to school; others resent or dislike personal conversations. Unless you know that a particular professor is open to chitchat, do not drop by his or her office to pass the time—you may actually make a bad impression. The professor may be doing research, writing, preparing for committee meetings, preparing or grading examinations, or organizing lectures. Of course, do not hesitate to visit the professor during office hours to seek any help you might need related to coursework or to advise him or her of personal situations affecting your attendance or the quality of your schoolwork. Some instructors, especially for lower-division courses, may prefer that you see their TA to discuss any routine business.

Textbooks

It is a good idea to buy textbooks before the first day of classes if possible. One practical reason for this is to avoid long lines. A more important reason is that you can look through the books and get a good idea of what the courses will cover. You can even begin reading the books to better prepare yourself for the courses. Check out your bookstore's refund policy to make sure you can return books should a class be cancelled or if the professor decides to change books at the last minute. Do not write in the book until you are sure you are going to keep it, and keep the bookstore receipt. Keep in mind also that if a book is shrink-wrapped, the bookstore might not take it back for the new book price if you remove the wrapping. When you do decide to keep a textbook, write your name and some other identifying information in it so that it can be returned to you if you lose it.

Textbooks are very expensive, so look after them. If you leave a book in a classroom or other places on campus, you may never see it again, because books can usually be sold back to the bookstore or other book buyers for a considerable amount of money. Also, be cautious about loaning your book to a fellow student, especially one whom you do not know well. I know of several cases in which books were loaned, the student to whom the book was loaned dropped the class, and the student who loaned the book never saw it again. Sometimes the instructor may have an extra copy of the book and be willing to loan it out, or the instructor may have put a copy or two of the book on reserve in the library. Books and other materials at the reserve desk of the library can be used in the library for a limited amount of time. Although they cannot be checked out, you could hand copy important information or photocopy it.

Consider the bookstore a place to explore. By browsing through books, you may find subjects that interest you, including those that you had not given a second thought to when you saw them listed in the catalog.

Creating a Textbook Library

You should sell your books back only if money is a major concern. If you have spent a term diligently studying a book, that book is now a familiar resource for you. Students often consult their textbooks from previous classes in current classes. For instance, textbooks from one class may give you ideas for term papers in another class. If a current class is related to a previous one, you can consult the text from the first course to clarify some basic ideas that have become fuzzy to you. It is especially important to keep books in your major (and minor). A library of familiar books can serve as best friends to an upper-division or a graduate student.

Computers

Personal computers have become as much a part of college education as textbooks, pens, notebooks, and professors. Much of the information that was in paper form in the past is now available online—sometimes *only* online. Entire textbooks or supplements for printed textbooks can be found online. In addition, course syllabi and other course information, entire courses (online courses), college and financial aid forms, databases of all types, reference materials, access to library resources, and means of communication (such as email and instant messaging) can be found online. It is therefore essential that you learn how to use the computer tools available to you. Most colleges have practical computer courses geared to train students to use computers as a research and communication aid. If you are not as computer literate as you should be, think about taking one or more of these courses. If you do not have your own computer, you can use one in your college's computer lab or other areas of the campus (such as libraries and residence halls) where computers are available to students.

The Internet

The Internet has been called the "information superhighway." Perhaps no other category of people can benefit more from a ride down that highway than students. If you do not have personal access to the Internet, your college will have computer labs that offer access. Public libraries also provide Internet access.

There is a vast amount of information on the Internet. One way to find the information you want is to use a uniform resource locator (URL). The URL is like an address. For instance, to reach the home page of the publisher of this book, Prentice Hall, you would type the URL http://vig.prenhall.com/. From there you can click on different menus or do a search of the site. One of the areas

If you do not have personal access to the Internet, your college will have computer labs that offer you access.

you could click on is "Browse our catalog." This would take you to a menu of subject areas and you could then click on "Student Success and Career Development." From there you could find the following topics to explore:

- Freshman Orientation/Student Success
- Study Skills
- Concise Student Success
- Critical Thinking
- Distance Learning
- Transition
- Career and Self Explorations
- Career Placement/Job Search
- Personal & Professional Development

A second way to gain access to a site on the Internet is to use a search engine. Search engines are programs that allow you to search for a subject by using a key word. For instance, on some search engines you would simply type "Prentice Hall" at the proper place and click on the search command, and the home page would come up on the screen. Some search engines are quite specific, such as Med-link, which allows you to search for information in the medical sciences. More general Internet search engines that search for a large range of data include Google, AltaVista, Excite, Yahoo!, and Lycos. The site called SearchEngineWatch (http://searchenginewatch.com/links/) lists and rates most search engines, giving the advantages and disadvantages of each.

Although the Internet provides a wealth of resources for students, it also contains a lot of "junk." Materials from sources such as online encyclopedias might be out of date. Just as printed materials might not be accurate, there is also no guarantee that material on the Internet is accurate. Therefore, stick to known entities, such as respected professional journals and information from reputable organizations, when doing your research.

Through the World Wide Web students can access numerous types of resources including

- information on colleges and universities
- course lectures from various universities
- academic discussion groups
- information on study skills
- information on books including publishers' catalogs and book reviews

- educational software

- online magazines and journals

- up-to-date news reports

- academic newsletters including ones that update textbooks

- study guides and online resource centers that accompany some textbooks

- tutorials for virtually any topic

- abstract services

- lab manuals

- glossaries, dictionaries, and virtually all other types of reference materials

- museum catalogs and collections

- online bookstores

- information on financial aid

- library holdings and services

- government databases

- state, city, and federal agencies

In addition to finding these resources, the Internet can be used to send and receive email, communicate with professors at your school or at another school, communicate with other students for such purposes as information sharing and participation in a study group, and communicate with experts in any field who work in a nonacademic setting.

This section has provided a very brief introduction to the Internet. To maximize your use of the Internet, you will have to have a more comprehensive understanding of it. Find out if your college teaches courses on the use of the Internet, or if your academic textbooks have sections on how to best use the Internet for their particular discipline. Keep in mind also that some Internet service providers have online guides to the Internet. Of course, there are numerous books on the use of the Internet that you can purchase or borrow from your school or local library. Here are few of them:

Bleck, Bradley W. *Navigating the Internet for Student Success.* Upper Saddle River, NJ: Prentice Hall, 2003.

Levine, John, Margaret Levine Young, and Carol Baroudi. *The Internet for Dummies.* New York: John Wiley & Sons, 2004.

Morkes, Andrew. *College Exploration on the Internet: A Student and Counselor's Guide to More Than 500 Websites.* Chicago: College & Career Press, 2004.

You can also consult the website Internet 101 at www.internet101.org/.

Why Do I Have to Take This Course?
The Goals of Liberal Studies

Here are two questions instructors often hear from students: "Why do I have to know all these facts?" and "Why do I have to take this course?" In other words: "What is the purpose of a broadly based liberal arts education?" Liberal studies or liberal arts and science education contrast to vocational or professional school education. Western universities require a liberal arts education for their undergraduate students for most majors (exceptions might be business, accounting, allied health, engineering, architecture, and some other majors). Liberal studies students must take classes in English, humanities (literature, the arts, and philosophy), history, foreign languages, social sciences, mathematics, and natural sciences. The liberal arts education is meant to provide students with broad knowledge, critical thinking abilities, and the skills to participate intelligently in the democratic process. The instruction provided to non–liberal arts majors at universities, graduate-level students at universities, and students attending vocational schools focuses on the skills and knowledge required for a specific occupation.

Liberal arts students often wonder why they have to know certain facts that are presented in lectures or textbooks. These facts include dates, names, statistics, and other information that students might think is overly specific or unimportant to their ultimate career goals. Furthermore, when students take courses that are not related to their majors, they might wonder about the relevance or value of these courses to their lives. For example, a student might think, "I am going to be an engineer, so why do I have to take a sociology class?" Indeed, much information that we receive might be perceived as not having a direct relationship to the things that currently interest us. Also, we might forget many of the things we learn—or at least they may be lost to conscious recall. However, *all information has the potential to be valuable and relevant.*

Data from studies support a number of hypotheses about learning and memory. However, a general scenario might be offered. Information is received by way of the five senses: sight, hearing, touch, smell, and taste. The information is transmitted to the brain, where it is compared with related knowledge that has been gained through previous experiences. The mind then creates an image or "story" to explain what a person has sensed. This process is continuous, automatic, and often completely subconscious.

This is where answers to the two questions at the beginning of this section come into play. The correctness and detail of the image that your mind creates about any received information is in large part due to the size of your mind's stored bank of experience and information. So, the more data that flow into your brain, the larger, more precise, more powerful, more creative, and more critical your mind will become.

Information from various areas of thought might help you to put apparently unrelated things into a variety of different perspectives. For example, an astronomy instructor might help students understand the relative distances between the sun and the planets (and relative sizes) by placing a soccer ball–sized "sun" at some point on the campus and other balls to scale throughout the campus. The instructor would then lead the students on a path from the "sun" to each of the "planets" while trying to maintain a view of the "sun." This experience would allow students to discover that some of the "planets" are smaller than the diameter of a pin compared to the soccer ball sun. To complete this exercise, the campus would actually have to be very large, since if done according to the actual scale of the solar system the outermost "planets" would be several miles from the "sun."

Once stored in the brain, this exercise provides a very dramatic experience that is available to help the student analyze other phenomena. For instance, students often have a hard time understanding evolution because they have no reference point to understand the meaning of time periods of tens of millions or even billions of years. However, by creating mental analogies of distance and time an image might emerge. That is, time can be equated to distance. We can say that a path from New York to Los Angeles represents the history of the earth. If New York represents 4.5 billion years ago and Los Angeles is current time, then, as we travel from New York to Los Angeles, the first life forms would appear in Indianapolis, Indiana, and the first animal life would appear in Phoenix, Arizona. The first primates would evolve at about Disneyland, 10 miles from the Pacific Ocean, and the first direct ancestors of humans would be evolving on the shore of the Pacific Ocean (see Exhibit 2.9).

Having the experience of "walking" through the solar system and sensing the relative distances and sizes of the sun and planets might also help to create a mental picture of the meaning of long stretches of time. These bits of information can be applied to other things that you learn and can help you to remember certain facts by making mental associations. One of the main reasons for a liberal arts education is to expand the mind so that new information can be analyzed in valid and creative ways.

While a professional or trade education can teach you to perform specialized tasks (plumbing, accounting, chemical analysis, biological illustration, and so on), a liberal arts education can prepare you to become a decision maker. In most jobs, as well as in daily life, choices are available: "What marketing strategy should be used on the target group?" "Should we have a second child, and if we decide to, when would be the best time?"

EXHIBIT 2.9   An example of a mental analogy of how one might equate time to distance.

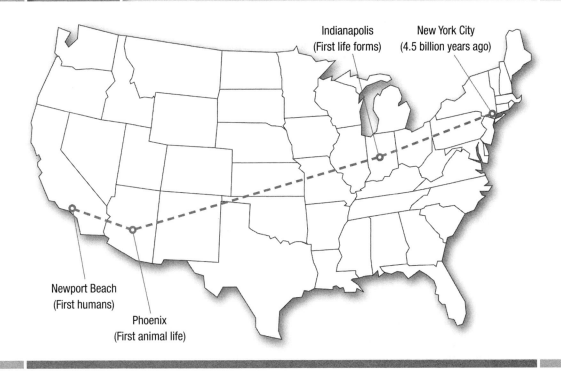

One of the traditional rationales justifying a liberal arts education has to do with such an education's potential to prepare a person to make sound political choices. Ideally, the strength of a democratic society depends on its citizens' ability to make wise choices about candidates and issues. A liberal arts education can provide you with the critical thinking abilities to make logical decisions based on concrete information, and it can also make it harder for people to convince you of false or misleading facts.

A liberal arts education also provides you with the flexibility that you might very well need to meet the challenges of a rapidly changing world. No longer can a person expect to be doing the same job in the same way for an entire career. With technologies and job markets quickly changing, a broad educational background will help you to deal with unexpected opportunities and changes and to cope with setbacks in your career(s). For further information on liberal studies, see

"Liberal Arts & Science Resources" at www.educationindex.com/liberal/

"The Role of Liberal Arts in Your Future" at www.iseek.org/sv/20005.jsp

"General Education in the Curriculum" at www.psu.edu/bulletins/bluebook/gened/ explains general education requirements and discusses the purposes of general [liberal] arts education.

A Note to Foreign Students and Nontraditional College Students

Many instructors have the attitude that an A is an A is an A. In other words, different criteria are not warranted for grading different types of students. This means that no allowances will be made for foreign students' difficulty with oral or written English. Such students should, therefore, improve those skills by taking a course or courses in ESL before taking other classes. In fact, such courses may be required for admittance depending on the results of assessment tests. Study skills or learning centers (discussed in Chapter 3) may also be helpful.

Assessment centers can also help nontraditional college students evaluate their present reading, writing, math, and other skills. Traditional students are people who enter college directly out of high school. Nontraditional students are older students who either never attended college as traditional students or are returning after an absence from college. Of course, all students should make themselves aware of prerequisites to a course. These might be official prerequisites listed in the catalog and schedule of classes, or they might be unofficial prerequisites based on the expectations of specific instructors. You might learn of these unofficial prerequisites from the instructor on the first day of class or from the class syllabus. Or you might learn of them from talking to other students who have taken courses by the instructor in the past. Realistically determine whether you have the necessary "equipment" to succeed in your classes.

Many schools have special counselors whose job it is to help foreign students and nontraditional students. If you fall into either of these categories, seek out these counselors. Also, find out if your college has special programs, tutors, and personal development classes for foreign and nontraditional students.

The website EduPass! The SmartStudent™ Guide to Studying in the USA is geared toward foreign students and has links to other sites that deal with college admissions, financing college, ESL, passports and visa requirements, cultural differences, living in the United States, as well as other links and resources. The site can be found at www.edupass.org/.

A quite comprehensive site called *Back to College* can be found at www.back2college.com/. It includes advice on a wide range of topics of interest to nontraditional college students as well as an online forum and a section called "Ask the Experts."

The site of the Association for Non-Traditional Students in Higher Education is an excellent resource for the "adult learner." It includes numerous useful links to other sites for nontraditional college students, including links to financial aid and scholarship sites, professional and student organizations for nontraditional students, honor societies, and other useful resources. You can find this site at www.antshe.org/.

A Note to Students with Disabilities

All colleges have an office that serves students with disabilities. Three federal laws and various state laws mandate that schools provide programs and services for the disabled: The Individuals with Disabilities Education Act of 1990 and its amendments of 1997, Title II of the Americans with Disabilities Act of 1990, and Section 504 of the Rehabilitation Act of 1973. You can access these laws through the Internet and should understand the rights that they provide to you.

The Disabled Student Services Office (which will have different names at different schools) might provide

1. various types of counseling.
2. academic adjustment programs and auxiliary aids and services (which might include placement tests, learning disability testing, special orientation programs, special classes, tutoring, testing accommodations for regular college classes, Braillewriter and Braille printers, print enlargers, sign language interpreters, note takers, on- and off-campus liaisons, and other programs and services depending on student needs).
3. priority registration.
4. mobility assistance.
5. priority housing registration and special housing accommodations.

Offices other than the Disabled Student Services Office such as counseling and career services offices or the health office might provide some services for disabled students. Each college might organize its disabled student services somewhat differently. Make sure you check out the programs and services available at your school and utilize the ones that will help you succeed.

The Virginia Department of Education puts out an 88-page booklet called *Virginia's College Guide for Students with Disabilities.* Although some of the information is specific to colleges in Virginia, most of the material is of general interest. The booklet includes sections on federal programs, financial aid and scholarships, and disability organizations. The booklet can be found on the Internet by simply typing in the title using a search engine.

Developing College Survival Skills

Stress Management

The pressure associated with getting good grades can be quite challenging at times, which makes stress management a relevant and important goal for the college student. There are numerous books on the subject, plus your college might offer stress management classes or workshops. Often psychology or physical education departments offer these classes. In addition, many colleges have crisis counselors who will be able to provide you with suggestions to relieve your stress. Here are some very general suggestions for managing stress:

1. Get sufficient sleep.
2. Learn about proper diet and apply what you have learned.
3. Exercise regularly in a way compatible with your general health.
4. Learn a relaxation method such as yoga.
5. Do not take on more activities than you know you can do successfully. Failure often leads to a reduction in self-esteem, which leads to tension, anxiety, and stress. Low self-esteem in turn often leads to low academic achievement. (For a review of information and research on self-esteem, see the website of the National Association for Self-Esteem at www. self-esteem-nase.org/research.shtml.)
6. Avoid mind-altering substances.
7. Schedule recreational or hobby activities into your week.
8. Manage your time efficiently. (See the next section.)

No books are listed here for this topic because a stress management program should be geared to the individual. Ask your doctor or other health specialist if he or she can recommend reading materials specifically in areas where you need self-improvement. Avoid popular self-help books on health unless someone with specialized knowledge in the health field has recommended them; these books are often faddish and could turn out to be more harmful than beneficial. Some popular but unsound diet books have caused death or illness in people who followed their advice. I provide here the relevant sections of two universities' websites that provide general information on stress management. However, if stress seems unbearable to you, you need to seek professional help from a doctor or licensed therapist.

"Stress and College Students" (University of Florida) at www.counsel.ufl.edu

"Managing Stress: A Guide for College Students" from the University Health Center and the University Stress Planning Group at the University of Georgia at www.uhs.uga.edu/stress/

Time Management

One of the most important college survival skills is effective time management. Many students have conflicting demands on their time from employment, family obligations, social activities, and schoolwork. Properly managed time is essential to reduce stress in such circumstances. But even for those students who are fortunate in not having many obligations outside of college, proper time management is extremely beneficial.

One simple but effective aid to time management is to carry an appointment calendar with you. This could be a paper calendar or an electronic device that provides a calendar. When dates of tests, review sessions, field trips, and so forth are announced, immediately enter them on your calendar. See what adjustments you must make on the basis of the newly announced dates. Exhibit 3.1 is an example of pages from a daily calendar.

In addition to an appointment calendar, on a sheet similar to the one shown in Exhibit 3.2 or on an electronic device, block out each known school activity as well as other activities in your schedule. Do this for each week, each month, and the entire semester. Write down your work schedules, the hours that you attend class, when you are going to visit your relatives, when you are going out socially—write down everything. Include new information, as it becomes known.

EXHIBIT 3.1   Three examples of daily calendars.

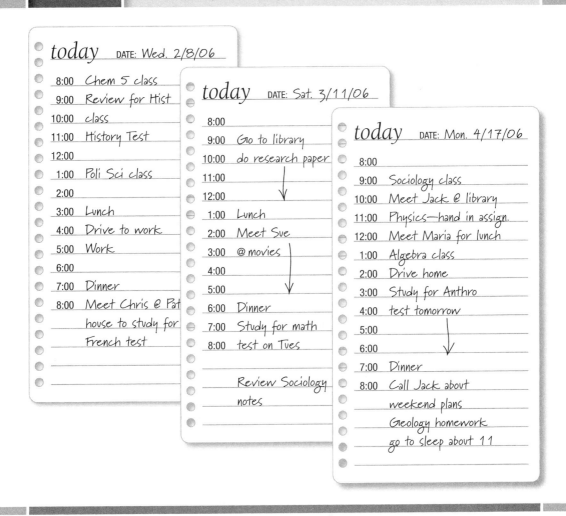

After you have done this, determine when you are going to study, write reports, visit professors during their office hours, and do other course-related activities. Apportion time for each course you are taking. Of course, you do not have to stick dogmatically to the schedule. Nor can you, since unexpected things do come up. However, if on a regular basis you see that your schedule does not allow enough time to prepare for your courses, you will know that you need to make changes. This may involve reducing the number of units you are attempting, cutting down on work hours, or altering your social schedule.

EXHIBIT 3.2   A typical weekly appointment calendar.

	MON	TUE	WED	THU	FRI	SAT	SUN
8							
9							
10							
11							
12							
1							
2							
3							
4							
5							
6							
7							
8							
9							
10							
11							

Even if you decide to forgo detailed scheduling on a regular basis, it is most important to organize your time for studying for exams and preparing papers—especially if you have to take several exams or turn in several papers in a short period of time. Analyze how much time you will need for each test and paper, and map out your study schedule for two to three weeks before this concentrated period.

From your calendar, construct a list of important dates like the following:

- November 1, Psychology 101 test
- November 5, Statistics midterm
- November 6, 3rd English paper due

Next, construct a more detailed list of exactly what you need to do to accomplish your goals:

- October 20—Finish Chapter 6 in psychology text—Do study guide test on Chapter 6—Call Jill—Make dentist appointment.
- October 21—Start Chapter 7 in psychology text—Do math problems 1–15 in Exercise 10—Work on sociology term paper—Write a letter to Aunt Sue.

For more information on managing your time, see

"Time Management" (University of Minnesota Duluth) at ccc.commnet.edu/faculty/~simonds/time.htm

"The Art of Time Management" (Capital Community College) at www.d.umn.edu/student/loon/acad/strat/time_manage.html

Using Study Skills Centers and Taking Study Skills Courses

Many schools have "walk-in" tutoring centers, such as a writing laboratory or a general study skills center, that can help students improve their reading and math skills, lecture note taking, and study habits. At these centers, students' skills are analyzed through testing and then tutors help students to overcome any problems. Study skills centers often include a library of books on reading, writing, math, and other academic skills, as well as tapes, filmstrips, and other aids. Workshops might also be available.

Many schools offer a variety of study skills courses. These courses may be found in personal development, psychology, English, math, or guidance departments. Consult your catalog or counselor about the availability of these courses at your college or university.

The following text provides hints on study skills. Personnel at your study skills center and the websites and books suggested offer additional and more comprehensive aid in each study skill area.

Taking Notes

According to one study, about 62 percent of what a student hears in class is forgotten within one day (Walter Pauk, *How to Study in College*, Houghton Mifflin, Boston, 1997). Taking good lecture notes is therefore always important. Even if the material covered in class is also covered in the text, your notes will indicate what points the instructor considers most important—and these points might be the ones emphasized on tests. Of course, it is even more important to take good notes in classes in which much of the material is covered almost exclusively during lectures.

What are good notes? They are notes that help you recall close to 100 percent of the lecture material. But this does not mean that you should attempt to write down everything. Unless you know shorthand, writing everything down would be impossible. It is also unnecessary to record everything, and attempting it will actually reduce your ability to understand the lecture. Good note taking generally requires that one balance listening with writing. If you spend all of your time attempting to get down every word, you might miss some very important points while detailing less important ones. Time spent listening allows you to grasp an overview of the material and thus identify the essential aspects of it. You are also able to catch subtle points that can be gleaned only from the instructor's nonverbal behavior such as facial expressions and tone of voice. Here are some pointers on taking notes:

1. **Abbreviate as much as possible.** Just make sure you use abbreviations that you will understand when you read over your notes (see Exhibit 3.3).

2. **Preread.** If applicable, read the material in the book that corresponds to a lecture *before* the lecture. This way you will know what material you can look up in the book (including spellings and definitions of words) should you miss writing it down. You can, therefore, concentrate your note taking on the material that is not covered in the text. This practice will also enable you to ask useful questions.

3. **Ask questions.** By asking questions you not only obtain answers that will help you understand the material, but you also participate in the class. Such participation can convert a class from an uninteresting or neutral experience to a stimulating and exciting one.

4. **Sit where the instructor can see you, and where you can clearly hear everything that is said.** Studies have shown that most classroom interaction occurs between the instructor and students sitting in the center of the classroom (see Exhibit 3.4).

5. **Outline the lecture rather than attempt to write notes in essay form.** An outline may give you a better understanding of the overall lecture and the relationship between one topic and another. There is no need to stick to any specific outline format. Use whatever technique you find comfortable. Instructors at a study skills center may be able to help you develop the best form for note taking.

EXHIBIT 3.3   Taking notes.

Two examples of notes are displayed. The first set of notes (a) was taken on a 10-minute stretch of a lecture and the second (b) on a 15-minute segment. Note the use of phrases, lists, underlining for emphasis, and abbreviations.

(a)

Major pollutants—AIR
  Carbon monoxide (CO)   Particulates
  Sulfur oxides   Nitrogen oxides
  Unburned hydrocarbons
  1. CO
    Largest single pollutant—50% of ALL
    Colorless, odorless, tasteless GAS
      —Mostly from cars   Also from cigarettes—individual
    acts on blood
    Competes with O2   Form strong chemical bond   see p 178 in book
  2. Sulfur oxides

(b)

HOW TO DO MOUTH TO MOUTH
1. Check for consciousness
    baby—flick cheek or foot—startle
    adult—gently—"hey, are you awake?"
  baby lying—almost no movement
  when asleep
2. Call for help—
    go for help & come back & tell me
3. Open airway—
4. Look, listen, & feel
    look at chest, listen for gasping
    wheezing, croaking sound
    feel w/ cheek for return of
    moist, warm air
    1—and, 2—and———5
  could be shallow breathing

5. 2 full breaths—baby—2 puffs
    over mouth & nose
  after 2 breaths—breath went in
6. Check for pulse—
    baby—brachial—5—10 secs
  If they have any pulse at all, you could
  put them into arrest
  better to wait for 10 secs if question
7. If any pulse at all, give breaths
    adult—1 breath @ 5 secs (12/min)
    child—1—8 yrs 1 breath @ 4 secs
    (15/min)
    infant—1 breath @ 3 secs (20/min)
    most humans—18—20/min
    with baby—don't tilt head too far
    tilt head just a little

EXHIBIT 3.4   Where to sit in a classroom.

Studies on elementary through high school grades show that students sitting in the zone emphasized in the illustration participate in classroom activities more than those sitting outside the zone.

6. **If necessary, slow down the instructor.** Most instructors will
repeat or clarify what they have said when asked.

7. **At home, as soon as possible after class, copy the day's notes
and make corrections.** Use the text (including the glossary if one exists),
dictionary, or other books to make your notes as complete and accurate as
possible. If you go over your notes on the same day, your recall of the material will be good and you can add things you heard but failed to write down.

8. **Attend class.** As far as understanding the content of a course, *there is no substitute for regular attendance.* However, if you must miss a class, ask another student who takes excellent notes if you can photocopy his or her notes. Review the notes given to you and ask the student to clarify any that you do not understand. Recopy the notes, changing the wording when necessary to make them more meaningful to you and adding anything you learned from questioning the student. You might even try borrowing the notes of more than one person. Or you could ask someone to tape the lecture for you (see "Using Recording and Other Devices" in this chapter).

It is easier to take notes on the lectures of some instructors than others, because some subject matter is more concrete than others and some instructors are better organized than others and put more effort into their delivery. Additionally, some instructors may have heavy foreign accents. If a lecture appears disorganized to you, or if the lecturer is hard to understand in other ways, ask plenty of questions, and even make a trip to the instructor's office during his or her office hours if necessary.

Many specific note-taking systems have been developed over the years. A page on the California Polytechnic State College study skills website called *Notetaking Systems* lists five popular methods of taking notes. It can be found at www.sas.calpoly.edu/asc/ssl/notetaking.systems.html. Also see

"Effective Notetaking Improves your GPA" (Seton Hill University) at http://jerz.setonhill.edu/writing/academic/notes2.htm

"Note-Taking Strategies: How to Get Your Class Notes into Shape" (College Board) at www.collegeboard.com/article/0,3868,2-10-0-955,00.html

"Note-taking" at www.hope.ac.uk/gnu/stuhelp/notes.htm

Participating in Class

In many non-American cultures, college students are expected to sit quietly and to talk only if directly asked to do so. The degree to which an American college professor will allow or desire students to ask questions spontaneously or participate in other ways will vary greatly. Yet it is common for American instructors to encourage their students' active participation in class. A lack of participation is likely to be interpreted as a lack of interest, motivation, or knowledge. So, if your instructor requests that students ask questions, bring in articles on topics being discussed, attend lectures by guest speakers, and take part in class discussions or debates, it would be wise for you to attempt to satisfy that request.

It is much more difficult for some students to be verbally active than others. However, developing one's participatory skills is important for classes that require such participation (e.g., upper-division or graduate-level seminars) as well as for many careers in which extroversion would be a definite positive.

When you do participate in class, follow the proper etiquette guidelines established by each instructor. This includes having a sense of when it is an appropriate time to make your contribution.

Using Recording and Other Devices in the Classroom

Writing good lecture notes forces you to put classroom information into your own language, using words, expressions, and symbols familiar to you. You might add notations on previous experiences, drawing on knowledge that is relevant to you, to help you remember the material and connect it with other information. Note taking is the first step in processing information—analyzing it, synthesizing it, determining what about it is most important, and organizing it.

To get the same value from a tape or other method of recording lectures, you would have to take notes from it as you listen. Since you do not need a record of everything that was said, this can be a waste of precious time. Thus, it is better to take good notes the first time you hear the lecture (in class) than to tape it and listen to the lecture twice.

There is another problem with recording lectures. If you put off listening to the tapes, at the end of three or four weeks, especially if you are doing this in several classes, you may have so many hours of tapes that you will not have enough time to listen to them. Then you will be entirely without notes.

Recording a lecture does, however, have several advantages. For example, if you are going to be absent from a class, you could have a friend record the lecture so that you will not have to depend on someone else's note-taking abilities. Remember to listen to the recording as if you were at the lecture and take notes. Also, recording a language class in which drilling on pronunciation is an element of the course can be beneficial.

Recording a lecture might be advantageous for people who have a hard time taking notes and concentrating on a lecture at the same time. However, as you listen to the recording, take notes and stop the recording as often as necessary to think about what the lecturer has said.

If you do use an audio recording device, always ask permission. Some instructors feel that their lectures are "copyrighted" material and they do not want them taped. Others feel inhibited by the presence of a tape recorder.

Many colleges and universities have rules governing the use of recording and other electronic devices. Some of these rules are aimed at protecting the instructor's intellectual property from piracy. Others are to designed to protect against and discourage cheating. Electronic devices such as cell phones (including Internet-enabled cell phones), personal digital assistants, and Internet-connected laptops have been used for cheating on tests. If a student is caught cheating (any type of cheating), that student may receive an F on the assignment or test on which he or she cheated and, in some cases, may be expelled from the college.

Professional Lecture Notes

Some schools allow professional note-taking services on campus. These companies usually employ upper-division or graduate students to take notes in popular lower-division courses, and the notes are sold to students enrolled in these courses. Using prepared lecture notes is generally a bad idea. It could discourage a real effort to avoid missing classes as a student rationalizes, "I can always get the notes." Consequently, classroom interaction between the student and the instructor, such as asking and answering questions, is eliminated—and such interaction is an important part of the educational process.

Another disadvantage of using prepared notes is that even if the student does attend each class he or she might tend not to take notes. As a result, the student is not thoroughly processing the material. Because the student has not included his or her own notations and memory devices in notes, it is more difficult for the student to remember the material.

Professional lecture notes can be helpful for one of the same reasons that recording may be beneficial. If you are absent due to illness or other reasons beyond your control, and you failed to ask anyone to record a lecture, then the prepared notes could be a blessing. If there is a note-taking service at your school, ask one of the employees of the service if you can purchase a specific lecture for a missed class.

The Importance of Reading Skills

Perhaps the most important study skill a student can possess is the ability to read with a high degree of comprehension. This ability correlates highly with success in college as well as outside of college.

Reading with a high degree of comprehension is one of the most important study skills you can possess.

Conversely, a main frustration for some students is their inability to understand the required reading for their courses.

A lack of reading skills is the fastest route to self-doubt about one's ability to succeed in college. The solution can be easy: take a course in reading skills. If no such course exists at your school, you might be able to attend a reading improvement program offered by the college's study skills center. Reading classes might also be available as evening classes at a local high school or community center. In any case, you will probably be given various reading skills tests to determine problem areas. For you to improve a skill, you must first know what it is that you are doing wrong.

Some colleges provide free tutors who can help you on a one-on-one basis. If your college has a community services or extension program, a reading skills class may be included there. Check the community services or extension catalog for information. Good reading skills will build self-confidence. Moreover, such skills help you to enjoy learning.

One general suggestion about improving reading skills is that you become a reading "junky." Practice may not make perfect, but it usually helps to refine a skill. If you have never been excited about reading, the best strategy to take is to choose carefully what you read. Select magazines and books on your hobbies or special interests. Most important, *get into the habit of reading*. You will find that this will be one of the most enjoyable habits you can have. If you are a slow reader, consider taking a speed-reading class.

What follows is not a comprehensive course on reading, but it does offer hints on how to read a textbook effectively.

Reading a Textbook

Textbooks should not be read as you would read a novel. Moreover, technical books (math, chemistry, electronics, etc.) should be read differently from nontechnical ones such as a social science book. Some general principles should be followed in reading all types of textbooks.

Most texts are written from the general to the particular. That is, a general statement is made and then specific examples are used to back it up. This is often accomplished at several levels. The introductory chapter may be a general overview of the entire book. The introductory paragraph to a chapter may be a synopsis of that chapter, and the topic sentence of each paragraph may be a general statement about the content of the paragraph. Therefore, the following method for reading a textbook organized in this manner is useful:

1. **Explore the entire book.** See how it is organized and what it has to offer. Does it have several levels of headings? If so, these headings would make a good outline of the book. As you read the book, you could use the survey in Exhibit 3.5 or write an outline on a separate piece of paper. This would help you to comprehend the overall organization of each chapter and how the subtopics are related to each other. (Some textbooks provide such an outline for you at the beginning of each chapter or in a printed or online study guide for the book.) What learning aids are included in the book? If key words are underlined, italicized, or in boldface, consider making a list of them for review. Sometimes they are already listed for you at the back of the book, and some study guides might list them or even provide flash cards for the terms. Also, see if the book has a glossary.

Many books have a list of learning objectives at the beginning of each chapter, a chapter summary, and end-of-chapter review questions. All of these items are meant to help you understand and remember the material in the text. Take advantage of them. Check as well for appendices at the end of the book. These

EXHIBIT 3.5   Surveying your textbook.

TEXTBOOK SURVEY

Instructions: Reproduce this textbook survey and do the survey for all of your textbook and supplementary readings. Do this survey before the semester begins or within the first week of each class.

Name of the textbook _____

Authors _____

Year of publication _____

If the publication date is not within the last couple of years, do you think this might be significant?

_____

Look at the Brief Table of Contents (if there is one) **and the detailed Table of Contents.** What is your impression of the book from the table of contents?

_____

_____

_____

Read the other front matter (preface, introduction, tour of the book, etc.). What type of learning aids does the book have (summaries, critical thinking questions, review question, exercises, marginal glossary, boldface terms, and so on)?

_____

_____

_____

Are there online resources? If so, what are they (sample tests, exercises, Internet links, and so on)?

_____

_____

_____

Does a CD accompany the book? If so, what is included on the CD?

_____

_____

_____

Is free access to a database included with the text?

_____

1

EXHIBIT 3.5   Surveying your textbook (continued).

TEXTBOOK SURVEY

What is the theoretical approach of the authors?

_____

_____

_____

What do the authors want you to learn from reading and studying the book?

_____

_____

_____

How is the book organized?

_____

_____

_____

Look at the end materials of the book.
Is there an end-of-book glossary?

_____

Are there appendices? If so, write down the topics.

_____

_____

Is there a list of references?

_____

What else is at the end of the book?

_____

_____

Now explore the entire book. Look at topic sentences, read captions of illustrations, look at the pictures, and note all of the features of the book. What is your impression of the book? How do you think the features of the book will help you learn the information within it?

_____

_____

_____

_____

_____

2

added materials are usually meant to enhance the material in the main body of the text or to add more detailed treatment of selected topics.

2. **Always read the preface and other front matter.** The preface and other front matter set the tone for the entire book. These features of the book often tell you what theoretical approach the author is taking. The preface might also tell you about some organizational features of the book that you did not discover for yourself. Some books even have a front section with various names such as "Tour of the Book" that lists and gives examples of the book's features.

3. **Apply the SQ3R (Survey, Question, Read, Recite, and Review) reading method.** This is a time-tested method of reading a text that can increase your comprehension and ability to recall textual material. Next, we will discuss the method in terms of reading a whole chapter or a major section of a chapter; however, you may find it more effective to apply it to very small sections of a chapter, such as the material found between one topic heading and the next.

SQ3R

The first step of the SQ3R method is to **survey** the chapter. Do not, at this point, underline in the book or take notes. Read the introductory paragraph completely, and then read each topic sentence of every paragraph. Look at the pictures and read the captions. Read "boxed" material and look at graphs and tables. Read any summaries. What you are doing is "exploring," getting a feel for what the material is about. By going through the chapter quickly, you will get an idea of its general scope. Thus, later, when you go over the chapter in more detail, if you are having a hard time understanding something on one page you will know where is it is elaborated on further in the chapter, and you can then go to that section, read the material, and then return to the previous page. Reading a text often requires this type of back-and-forth treatment (see Exhibit 3.5).

The second step in the process of studying a text is to **question**. This step, which involves formulating questions while skimming, has proven highly effective for many people. Turn headings, topic sentences, or even captions to illustrations into one or more questions. For instance, the heading "The Four Ways Heat Is Transferred" could be converted into the question, "What are the four ways that heat is transferred?" Or the illustration caption "Types of Cell Division" could be turned into the questions, "How many types of cell division are there?" and "How do these stages of cell division differ from each other?" These questions can be written down as one skims the chapter.

The third step is to **read** the chapter thoroughly, word for word, outlining important points as you go along. You can underline or highlight directly in the book or make an outline of the chapter on a separate sheet of paper. Or, you can highlight the book in such a way that it allows you to easily go back and make an outline or write note cards. Because you are forced to process the information (organize, analyze, and summarize it), outlining is better than just underlining or highlighting. Always look up unfamiliar words in the dictionary (or in the book's glossary if it has one). Misinterpretation of a single word could lead to a misunderstanding of an entire idea.

The fourth step can be done after the "read" step or simultaneously with it. It is called the **recite** step. While or after reading each chapter or section of a chapter, recite or write answers to the questions that you formulated while skimming. These questions form your own personal guide. When applicable, try to come up with your own examples of the subjects discussed or additional insights into the material being covered. Check the answers to your questions against the material in the book. If you cannot answer the questions satisfactorily, reread the textual material.

The final step is to **review** your knowledge of the material that you have been studying. Look over any notes that you have taken. Go over material that you have underlined and/or highlighted in the book. If you can, get someone to ask you questions based on your notes. Write elements in the chapter that you are having a difficult time memorizing on flash cards and carry them with you so you can review them at any time. Review your notes, highlighted and/or underlined text, and flash cards immediately before a test. If there is a study guide that provides tests and answer keys, take those tests and check your answers. Many books, especially for introductory-level courses, now have online learning resources with tests. When you take these tests, the computer will usually score them for you. In some cases, if you provide an incorrect answer to a question, the computerized response will include feedback that will tell you why the answer is wrong.

Additional Suggestions for Reading

Some other pointers on reading textbooks are as follows:

1. **Avoid moving your lips when you read.** This has been shown to cut down on reading speed.

2. **Draw a finger across the page under sentences to help you read faster.** When doing this, make sure you still read the material word for word.

3. **Do not read everything at the same pace.** Easily understood material can be read faster than complex material. In fact, you may have to read some passages several times in order to comprehend their meanings.

4. If exercises or self-quizzes at the end of the chapter are not assigned, read them anyway. They provide a good check of your understanding of the material. If answers are not provided, check your work with the instructor, tutors (schools often provide free tutoring), or even other students who have done the work.

5. Use study guides and online resources. If available for your text, purchase and use a study guide to test further your comprehension and retention of the subject matter. If your instructor does not assign a study guide, ask your instructor, the textbook's publisher, bookstore personnel, or Internet booksellers if one is available. A list of online booksellers can be found at www.biglion.com/bookstores-online.html.

Many textbooks have their own web page with the online resources. These resources might include an online learning center that provides a study guide with a variety of different types of tests, exercises, PowerPoint presentations, flash cards, Internet links to sites related to the topics of each chapter, and other resources. Always take advantage of these pedagogical aids.

6. If possible, personalize the material in the book. Have you personally experienced some of the things that the author or authors are discussing? If so, try to relate these experiences to the material in the book.

Textbooks must be studied, not just read, so be prepared for a time-consuming task. Experience, however, sharpens your skill in using textbooks and it will also increase your efficiency and speed. The two survey sheets in Exhibit 3.5 may be helpful to you in analyzing textbooks.

It should be noted that many textbooks provide free limited-time access to research tools such as Infotrak and Academic Search Elite (EBSCO). These resources can help you research information for papers. They are often also provided through the college library and are discussed in this chapter in the section called "Using the Library." See also "How to Read a Textbook" by Karen Fenske (Kishwaukee College) at http://online.kishwaukeecollege.edu/tips/sq4r.html.

Concentration

Many students have problems concentrating on studying for exams or listening to lectures. Although outside distractions are usually blamed, research shows that it is the way students interpret distractions that disrupts their study. What is a distraction to one student may not be to another. *Concentration* is the mental activity of directing your efforts and attention toward a specific goal, physical activity, problem, or topic. It is the ability to focus on something. Concentration aids memory. The section that follows discusses memory.

Here are some suggestions on how to improve concentration.

1. **Choose a place in a classroom or lecture hall with the least distractions.** Often this is in the front of the class. If you sit in the back of the class you will be able to see everything your classmates are doing and per-haps be distracted by it. You might be less distracted by noise in the front of the classroom. At least by being closer to the lecturer, you might hear what he or she is saying more accurately than if you sat farther away. Avoid sitting near fans, air-conditioning units, open doors, or other areas of a classroom that might be noisy or provide distractions.

2. **Directly after a lecture, review what you just heard.** This process works well for many people—if you immediately go over your lecture notes you might recall gaps in those notes that you can fill in before you forget the mate-rial. Also, you can write questions for the professor or TA on material that you need clarified. If your course has review, tutorial, or quiz sessions, look imme-diately in advance of those sessions at the material that is going to be covered.

3. **Create an environment appropriate for studying.** If possible, des-ignate a place that is to be used exclusively for studying. Make sure you have all the tools you need, including reference books, in this area. Control noise and the visual environment to acceptable levels. Create a work atmosphere as opposed to a recreational one.

4. **Choose the best times to study.** Study when you are most alert. This will vary from person to person. Some people are morning people and some are afternoon or night people when it comes to alertness and readiness to take on difficult tasks. It is always best to study when the fewest competing activities are in progress.

5. **Explore other ways to increase your concentration.** Become intensely involved with what you are studying. Keep a pad of paper handy to jot down extraneous thoughts that cross your mind while studying so you can get on with the task at hand. Set up goals as to how many pages, the number of problems, and so on that you want to do during each period of study and then reward yourself when you meet those goals. Boredom can disrupt one's ability to concentrate. Break up the content of study by mixing up subjects and building in variety and interest. Make the most of rest periods by doing something quite different from studying. Start with short study periods and

slowly build to longer periods only as fast as you maintain concentration. However, do not constantly look at a clock; this can be very distracting.

Remembering What You Hear and Read

As you take notes on a lecture or read a chapter from a textbook, your goal is to remember the material. If you have a problem accomplishing this, you might want to take a memory course or read a book on the topic of memory enhancement. Some other suggestions for improving retention follow.

As you read, try to tie in your preexisting knowledge to make the information more relevant to you.

People remember things that they can associate with existing experiences and knowledge better than isolated facts. So, if you have some familiarity with the subject in question, attempt to tie in your preexisting knowledge or your own personal examples or experiences. This will make the topic relevant to you. If this is not possible, try to come up with your own examples. In a physics class, if the instructor gives an example of the relationship between temperature and pressure, think of other possible examples of the same phenomenon or try to correlate the phenomenon to some other phenomenon. For instance, if you know that as the demand for a product goes up the price usually also goes up, you might make a mental correlation between this fact and the fact that as temperature goes up, so does pressure.

Try to relate experiences and correlate ideas whenever you can. There are numerous specific mnemonic (memory) techniques you can learn. For example, to remember the position of items in a list, make up some silly saying using the first letter or letters of each word. Suppose you want to commit the following epochs (a stretch of geologic time) of the Cenozoic Era (a larger unit of geologic time) to memory:

- Recent
- Pleistocene
- Pliocene
- Miocene
- Oligocene
- Eocene
- Paleocene

You might make up a sentence like, "Roy picked Peter mostly oily Eastern peanuts." The sentence you construct does not have to make sense—not even to you. It just has to be something that you will remember. Remembering RPPMOEP will keep these seven terms for the epochs of the Cenozoic Era in the correct order.

You will notice that there are three Ps in our example. How can you distinguish among them? One way might be to look up the word derivations in a regular etymological dictionary. Thus, the meaning of *Pleistocene* is "most new," and the Pleistocene is the "newest" (most recent) of the three "P" epochs. *Paleo-* means "ancient," and the Paleocene is the oldest of the "P" epochs. Pliocene is the remaining "P" epoch.

Every time you learn a Latin, Greek, or other root or affix used in English, you increase your potential to remember words and to figure out the meaning of words that you have never seen before. Spending some time learning

Latin and Greek forms is well advised. Appendix A provides a short course in the value of this technique.

To continue our example of geologic time, suppose you are required to know what important events occurred in each epoch. You could make up non-sense associations like using the "Pal" in Paleocene. You might say that primates are your pals and that they began to evolve just before the Paleocene, or you might even use rhyming association when applicable. The Pleistocene was the epoch in which the most recent ice ages took place, and "pleis-" rhymes with ice.

If you do not need to know the order of a series of facts, you can list the facts and take off the first letter or syllable of each. Then you can rearrange these letters or syllables into a word. Such a word, called an acronym, may help you remember the facts that you are trying to learn. For instance, if you need to remember the Great Lakes, the acronym "HOMES" might be con-structed. Each letter of the acronym is the first letter of lakes Huron, Ontario, Michigan, Erie, and Superior.

Making up or learning established mnemonic rhymes is another method of remembering. The best known of such rhymes, perhaps invented in 1562 by Richard Grafton, is

> "Thirty days hath November, April, June, and September, February hath twenty-eight alone, And all the rest have thirty-one."

Flash cards, an old standby, are especially helpful in learning large amounts of related material, such as a series of mathematical formulations, foreign words, linguistic symbols, and biological terms. Exhibit 3.6 gives an example of how flash cards can be set up. The websites for some textbooks allow students to print flash cards from the site.

The best way to remember anything is to understand it. If you know the rationale behind an idea, you are more likely to remember it and how it relates to other phenomena. When you read a book or listen to a lecture, ask questions (of yourself or the professor). Continually relate one thing you have learned to other things, creating a pattern of relationships. Work in study groups with other students to formulate questions to ask each other; some-times others will come up with an angle you did not think of. In addition, their questions to you may focus you in directions that you had not explored. The more complete your understanding of a topic, the easier it will be for you to remember specifics related to that topic.

Ask yourself and your instructors about the things that you are hearing and reading. Go over and over the material that is most difficult to you. Review the material for a test right before the test. If the test covers a lot of information, reduce the information to a page or two of the most important terms, formulas, and concepts. To do this, it might be helpful to pretend that

EXHIBIT 3.6   Example of a flash card.

One side shows the English word and the other side the German equivalent.

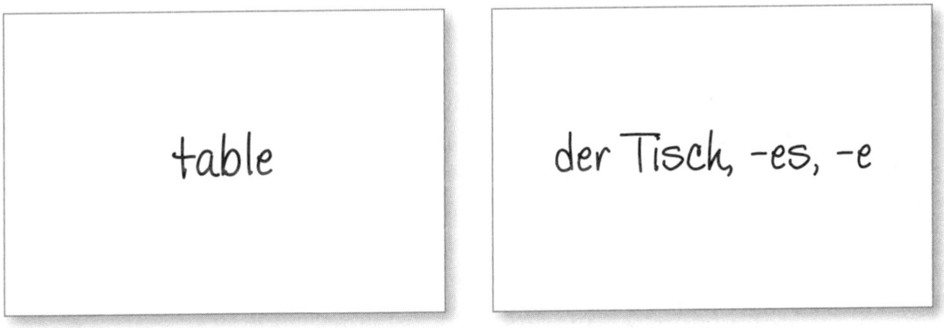

table

der Tisch, -es, -e

an instructor is going to allow you to bring a sheet or two of notes to a test. Then construct the sheet or sheets as if you could use them during the test. By condensing the material to its essentials, you will have to make an assessment of what is most important, organize the material to show how one fact relates to another, and use acronyms and other memory devices. The completed sheet or sheets can then be used to review for the examination.

The Dartmouth study skills web page called Where to Study/How to Study provides good information on many areas of study skills. The section on concentration and memory is especially useful and provides a more detailed treatment of memory enhancement methods. You can find it at www.dartmouth.edu/~acskills/success/study.html. Also see

"The Brain from Top to Bottom" at
www.thebrain.mcgill.ca/flash/a/a_07/a_07_p/a_07_p_tra/a_07_p_tra.htm

Ohio University's AAC *Study Tips on Memory* at
http://studytips.aac.ohiou.edu/?Function=Memory

Studying for and Taking Exams

nstructors almost universally see exams as valid measures of a student's understanding of a subject. Unfortunately, exams also measure how well a student takes exams. Just as a doctor, for example, develops skills in medicine, a student must develop skills in test taking in order to achieve the highest level of success possible.

Test Anxiety

Test anxiety is a feeling of worry and nervousness while studying for and taking examinations. Some anxiety is normal. However, if the anxiety is uncontrollable and, therefore, prevents you from learning the course's material and successfully taking tests or doing other assignments, you might need to seek professional help. Your college's counseling center might provide licensed therapists who can help you deal with this problem. For most students the best way to manage text anxiety is to be prepared for the test. Following are some tips on how to study for and take tests effectively. For a discussion of test anxiety, see "Test Anxiety" at www.counsel.ufl.edu or "Managing Test Anxiety" at www.sdc.uwo.ca/learning/mcanx.html.

Studying for Exams

Before studying for an exam, try to be aware of what your professor expects from you. Some instructors are more interested in detail than others. Some expect a relatively sophisticated understanding of a topic even at the freshman level. But how do you know what the first test in a class is going to be like? If your instructor gives a sample test or very detailed advance instructions, your task of preparation will be much easier. However, some instructors give little indication of the way they make up tests. In this case, you can take action in the following manner:

First, find out if the instructor will allow you to look at back tests. Some even provide the library with copies of back tests. Though the questions are not the same as the ones that you will be answering, they will show you what style of questioning the instructor uses.

Second, ask former students of the instructor about his or her testing methods. It is best to get several opinions, because each student may have a different perception of the instructor's methods. Tricky questions to one might be straightforward to another. If your school provides tutors, you might be able to find a tutor who has taken a class from an instructor of one of your current classes. If the instructor is using the same types of test, that tutor would be able to give you some insights into the instructor's testing methods.

Third, since many instructors take questions directly from study guides, see if an online or published study guide is available for the text that you are using. Ask your professor, check the textbook preface or back cover, or do an Internet search for supplements to the book. You can order the study guide from the publisher, through a bookstore, or through an online bookseller. Here are some additional hints on studying for tests:

1. **Do not procrastinate.** For most people learning gradually results in better retention than cramming.

2. **Organize your time.** If you have several tests to study for, divide your time according to a logical plan on paper. Even if you cannot stick to the plan exactly, you can gauge how well you are coming along. (See "Time Management" in this chapter.)

3. **Look up words you do not know.** Words can be looked up in a dictionary, in a book glossary, or online. In fact, on the search engine called Google, all you have to do is type in the word *define* and then the word you want defined into the search box and definitions from various sources will automatically be displayed. A word is more than a label; it embodies a concept. When you skip over words you do not know, you are skipping some of the content of the material that you are studying.

4. **Review lecture and text notes on a regular basis.** In class, ask questions based on these reviews. Make flash cards for specific information such as technical terms, formulas, and foreign words (see Exhibit 3.6).

5. **Make up your own questions and then answer them.** If you are having a test that involves problem solving, attempt to figure out what questions the instructor might ask and then prepare detailed answers. The same technique is good for true/false, multiple-choice, short-answer, and essay questions. There are a limited number of questions that an instructor who sticks to the subject matter can ask. As a "professional" student, one of your jobs is to anticipate those questions by determining which segments of the course material are of greatest importance. This technique brings you to the test well prepared to write thorough answers in the time provided, because you have already thought through your answers.

6. **Compare lecture and textual material on the same topic.** Comparing material on the same topic from different sources helps to build a general overall understanding of the material. If the two sources are ever in disagreement on an area, point this out to your instructor and ask for clarification.

7. **Do not proceed to the next topic until you understand the one you are studying.** When you need extra explanation, avail yourself of your instructor's office hours, study groups, the library, and any opportunities to ask questions in class.

8. **Try to study at times when you are alert.** Of course, this is not always possible for the student with numerous responsibilities.

9. **Prepare for the specific type of test that you will be taking.** Tests in mathematics, linguistics, foreign language, logic, and some science courses often emphasize problem solving. Preparation thus may involve repetitive drilling in particular types of problems. Several series of problem-solving books are provided in Appendix B. For students having a difficult time in a problem-solving class, these books (which usually include hundreds of solved problems) can make a significant difference. Preparing for a math or science test can also be aided by drawing diagrams that show the relationship of one factor (variable) to another (see Exhibit 3.7). When verbal models fail, visual models of a phenomenon sometimes provide insight into a problem.

Many college examinations are made up of multiple-choice and/or true/false questions (objective tests). Other tests are composed of short-answer or essay questions (subjective tests). Conventional wisdom might suggest that one should study differently for subjective and objective tests. Yet, at least one study has placed doubt on that notion. Some students were told to expect an essay examination whereas others were told to expect a multiple-choice test. Both groups were given a test with both types of questions.

EXHIBIT 3.7   Visualizing information.

One way to learn information is to convert it into a diagram such as (a), which shows the relationship of variables that apply to evolutionary theory, or a simple graph such as (b), which shows the relationship of income to education level.

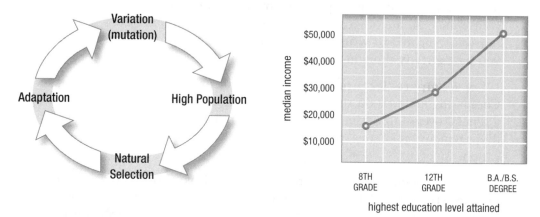

The students who studied for the essay exam performed better overall and even performed better on the multiple-choice questions than those who studied for the multiple-choice test. Therefore, the most practical advice is to *study for all tests as if they are going to be essays*. This means trying to gain an overall understanding of the material studied, rather than just memorizing facts.

10. **When studying, avoid distractions.** Radio, television, telephone calls, and noisy environments will disturb your concentration.

Taking the Exam

Be prepared to take an examination well before it is scheduled. The only preparation that you should have to do the night or morning before the test is to review for it. Go over your notes and underlined and/or highlighted sections of the text, review any mnemonic devices you have invented, and so on. A little nervousness before a test might create a feeling of being "up" for the test and have a positive effect. However, for those students who become excessively nervous before and during a test, the following suggestion might prove helpful: Do not study the night before the test. Indeed, that night avoid any thoughts of the test. Instead, study two days before the test is actually scheduled. Then, on the eve of the test, go to a movie or do something else relaxing. This is the opposite of cramming. Psychologists have found that as some people continue to cram they actually lose information. This leads to the familiar response after a test, "I went blank." Often once the test is over and the student relaxes, he or she begins to remember the blocked information. Although the preceding approach may help some people, reviewing the material as close to test time as possible is the best strategy for most students.

On essay or short-answer tests, if the question or questions being asked have more than one part, remember to answer all of the parts. If the question asks you to evaluate, do not summarize. In fact, there are a number of directive words of which you should understand the meaning. Some of these are as follows:

1. *Explain* means to make clear; interpret; clarify; tell the meaning of; or tell how to do something.
2. *Summarize* means to give concisely the main points of a topic.
3. *Evaluate* means to give the good points and the bad points; appraise; give an opinion regarding the value of; or discuss the advantages and limitations of something.

4. *Contrast* means to bring out the points of difference between two or more things.

5. *Define* means to give a meaning of a word or concept; or place it in the class to which it belongs and set it off from other items in the same class.

6. *Compare* means to bring out points of similarity and points of difference.

7. *Describe* means to give an account of; tell about; or give a word picture of something.

8. *Discuss* means to talk over; consider from various points of view; or present the different sides of something.

9. *Criticize* means to state your opinion of the correctness or merits of an item or issue. Although the word *criticize* connotes a negative opinion, a point of criticism can be positive or negative.

10. *Justify* means to show good reason for; give your evidence; or present facts to support your opinion of some issue or idea.

11. *Trace* means to follow the course of; follow the trail of; or give a description of the progress of something.

12. *Interpret* means to make plain; give the meaning of; give your thinking of; or translate something.

13. *Prove* means to establish the truth of something by giving factual evidence or logical reasons for something.

14. *Illustrate* means to use a word picture, a diagram, a chart, or a concrete example to clarify a point. (This list is adapted from Joan McGuire, ed., *The Shortest Distance to Learning: A Guidebook to Writing Across the Curriculum*, Los Angeles Community College District and University of California, Los Angeles, 1983, 52–53.)

Preparing properly for a test and following the directions for the test are essential for success. Here are a number of additional hints on test taking:

1. **Eat right.** You have probably heard this since elementary school days: "Eat your breakfast!" What was true in the second grade is just as true in college. Studies have repeatedly shown that good nutrition at proper intervals is critical to good concentration and performance. Students who do not eat breakfast might become inattentive and careless in the late morning.

2. **Try to get to school early on the day of the test.** Rushing to get to class will only serve to raise your level of anxiety.

3. **Look over the entire test as soon as you receive it.** See how many sections and what types of questions there are on the test. Determine

whether some questions are worth more points than others. Gauge your time so that you will be able to finish the test.

4. **Remember that on true/false tests, an answer is true only if the statement is always and completely true.**

5. **Read all of the entries on a multiple-choice test and judge the truth of each entry as if it were a true/false question.**

6. **On true/false and multiple-choice questions, first answer the questions that you know.** Be careful not to fill in the line on the answer sheet that you wanted to leave blank with the answer to the next question. If you put a mark next to questions that you skipped, make sure that the mark is not in the answer grid. If it is and you forget to erase it, the machine that grades the test may pick it up as an answer and mark the question wrong. After you have answered all of the questions that you are reasonably sure you know, go back and answer the ones that you skipped. You may now feel less rushed and some of the questions that you did answer may help you to answer the questions that you were unsure of the first time around. If you do not know an answer, make your best guess. If you do not answer a question, you will definitely not get credit for it. If you guess, you will have a chance to get that credit. (Some instructors may have grading systems that take more points off for wrong answers than for skipped questions. In this case, you might not want to guess at answers.)

7. **Mark answers on the answer sheet for an objective test lightly at first.** It is sometimes hard to erase very dark marks. Then when you are confident that your marks are your final answers, darken them.

8. **Check answers and change if necessary.** Conventional wisdom suggests that you should not change answers and that your first response is most likely to be correct. Controlled studies do not validate this notion. The result of one study* was that about two and a half times as many test answers were changed from wrong to right than the other way around. Of course, if you have enough data from your own past tests, you might want to analyze those tests to see what the best strategy might be for you in regard to changing answers.

9. **Outline and organize your answers.** For short-answer and essay questions, spend some time organizing your answer before you begin the

---

*Benjamin, L., Cavell, T., Shallenbergen, W. (1984). "Staying with Initial Answers on Objective Tests: Is It a Myth?," *Teaching Psychology*, 11(3), 133–141.

finished product. One way of doing this is to outline your answer. Do this on scratch paper if the instructor allows it, or do it at the top of the sheet on which you are going to write your short answer or essay.

10. **Take open-book tests seriously.** Students often hope for open-book tests and/or open-note tests. Yet, depending on the instructor's expectations, these tests can be as demanding or more demanding than closed-book and closed-notes tests. Open-book and open-note tests might be more complex in terms of critical thinking requirements and the level of highly specific information required.

When you hear "open-book test" do not think, "Oh, I don't have to study for this test." You need to carefully go through your book, flagging important pages so that you can find information very quickly. If you can also bring notes to the test, create outlines of the information that you believe will be on the test and write down essential things such as definitions and formulas on a separate sheet of paper. You could even write page numbers next to important definitions or topics in your notes.

Since you will have written resources with you, the instructor might ask more questions or questions that require longer answers than the instructor would ask on other types of tests. Therefore, one of the biggest factors in an open-book test is having enough time to complete it. If you come to the test having made no advanced preparations, you may spend so much time looking through the book for information that you will not have enough time to finish the test.

11. **Write neatly.** You do not want to lose points just because the professor cannot read your writing.

12. **Bring the proper equipment.** This may include pencils, erasers, a pencil sharpener, pens, rulers, answer sheets, or whatever else is required or can be used.

13. **Refrain from rushing through a test to get home early.**

14. **If you miss a test, make sure you know what the makeup procedure is.**

15. **If you are a student with disabilities, plan ahead when needed.** If you have arranged for accommodations such as taking tests at a different location such as a special services office, make sure you are aware of the procedure to follow. You might have to inform the instructor a certain amount of time in advance of the test and make arrangements for the test to be at the special services office.

Sample Essay Tests

Two essay tests taken at the same time are reproduced here. Both students had the same amount of time to complete the test. Neither was absent when the material was discussed in class. (Of course, even if a student is absent, it is his or her responsibility to get lecture notes for the days missed.)

Because you may never have taken a physical anthropology or biology class, you may not be able to judge the content of the answers given in the examples. But the contrast is so great that you will be able to make some judgments. Compare these and then read the discussion that follows the essays.

ANTHROPOLOGY 101 TEST 2—ESSAY (SAMPLE ONE)

Humans are animals, chordates, vertebrates, mammals, and primates. What are the main characteristics of each of these taxonomic categories?

Animals are differentiated from plants by various characteristics. Animals cannot synthesize their food from inorganic material like plants do, but must ingest other organisms. Most animals are highly mobile and have constricting tissues such as muscle. Animals are able to respond to their environment because they possess nerve cells and sensory mechanisms. Animals intake oxygen and emit waste in the form of carbon dioxide.

Chordates have internal skeletons and an important feature known as the notochord. The notochord is a backbone of sorts and dorsal to it (in back of it) is the nerve chord. In chordates, the nerve chord is single and hollow, as opposed to double and vertical like in anthropods. At some point in a chordate's life the organism possesses gill slits. Early chordates were filter feeders, forcing water through their gills to filter out particles of food. Vertebrates have a true spine or vertebral column.

Vertebrates developed bone in place of cartilage. Early vertebrates were also filter feeders. Agnathans, jawless vertebrates, survive today in the form of highly specialized organisms called lamprey and hagfish. Vertebrates developed jaws. The jaws didn't just come to be, they formed from existing structures called gill ??. Jawed vertebrates could attack and feed upon other organisms so they flourished. There were two kinds of early jawed vertebrates, placoderms, now extinct, and chondrichthyans (cartilaginous fish) that are represented today by sharks and rays. In freshwater vertebrates were bony fish (osteo something or other). Fish that were suited for drought conditions were crossopterygians. Crossopterygians had the ability to supplement their oxygen supply if a body of water became stagnant by use of primitive lungs. It was from crossopts that amphibians arose.

Amphibians were (and are) able to survive outside of the water but are closely tied to the water because wet skin allows them to breath and their eggs need water to survive. With the development of the amniotic egg came full-time land dwellers. The amniotic egg, an egg with a shell, allowed these animals to reproduce away from water. I skipped the fact that these organisms developed legs. The crossopterygians had bony structures in their fins. It was a selective advantage for these organisms, in time of drought, to be mobile enough to move from a drying up pond to a suitable body of water. Full-time land dwelling animals are called reptiles, and it was the reptiles that gave rise to mammals.

The first mammals that came to be were called synapsids and came very early in reptilian radiation. While synapsids were reptiles they had distinct mammalian characteristics and are sometimes referred to as mammal-like reptiles. While reptiles are said to be cold-blooded, they are poikilothermal. That is to say that their body temperature changes with outside temperature. Reptiles do what is known as behavioral thermoregulation. That is, they have to adjust their body temperature to a range where vital functions can be performed. They do this by hiding underground when it's cold or in shade when it's hot. Mammals are homiothermal. That is, their body temperature is constant. To keep their temperature constant, mammals have fur to keep warm, sweat glands to cool off, and mammals must intake a considerable amount of food (compared to reptiles) to keep warm.

Mammals have what is known as heterodont dentition. Their teeth are differentiated for different uses (i.e., cutting tearing, crushing). While reptiles have one kind of teeth that can be constantly replaced, mammals have only two sets, deciduous and permanent. Mammals nurse their young on milk produced in mammary glands. Mammals' young are born more developed because of internal development, and have close bonds with at least one parent. The exception is prototherians, egg-laying mammals represented today by echidnas and platypuses. Mammals have four-chambered hearts that allow oxygenated blood to be separate from deoxygenated blood. (Therians—marsupials—young develop slightly within the mother, are born and crawl into their mothers' pouches for further development.) Kangaroos are an example of therian mammals. Eutherian mammals have a placenta that allows maternal blood direct contact with the baby's blood, thus increases developmental efficiency.

Primates have 3-D color vision, pentadacty (five fingers) clavicle (collar bones allowing greater mobility) tactile pads (nerve endings in the fingers that are highly sensitive) and nails to protect the nerves. All of the mechanisms are suited for arborialism (living in trees). Primates can grasp with great strength. Primates have large, developed brains and complex behavioral patterns that some of which are learned through an extended childhood. Primates have decreased olfactory sense (sense of smell) probably because scent lingers near the ground, not in the trees.

ANTHROPOLOGY 101 TEST 2—ESSAY (SAMPLE TWO)

Humans are animals, chordates, vertebrates, mammals, and primates. What are the main characteristics of each of these taxonomic categories?

Chordates; symmetrical bodies, gill slits, cartilage plates. these animals are filter feeders that use there muscles to gyrate food into these elongated bodies, Like a tube. these were deep water beings that eventually rose to the surface. these were the jaw-less ancestors to the boney fish. they had teeth but only to latch on to its victim. eventually the gill slit moved upward forming a gill bar and a premature jaw thus arose into the vertebrates.

Vertebrates; these are also filter feeders, filtering its food. the vertebrates arose a boney fish. having transformed its carbide plates into solidified bone. the vertebrates over time started to leave the water to lay its eggs, the amniotic egg was an egg w/a shell allowing the vertebrates to move around. this is where the amphibians came from forming legs eventually (the frog) but still needing that H20 to enable them to survive, water on there skin allows them to breath so they don't dry up. Reptiles arose also from amphibians, having legs this allowed them to travel further in land, (Puddle jumpers) to a new environment. These are cold blooded animal mammals; are a very distinct group the only warm-blooded animals (Homo thermal) and the only animals that use the placenta for birth. it's more of a mother child relationship, the mother feeding through the mammary glands (for milk)—the mammals traveling to different environments make new and different subspecies through geographic isolation. Primates; are the latest to evolve. old and new world monkeys.

Primates have a distinct form. using there keen vision (stereoscopic) vision, and sense of smell. these animals are adapted to climb in the trees using there 5 finger digits to grasp, along with the use of there thumb for grasping (the Big toe also) these primates are much more intelligent than anything preceding them. They are very flexible animals allowing them to adapt quite easily to different environments. there are two main groups of Primates deciduous teeth Primates and permanent teeth Primates).

Analysis of Sample Essay Tests

Even to those unfamiliar with the subject matter, general differences between these sample tests should be apparent. Certainly the writing ability displayed in the second test is far below that of the first. A question instructors often hear from students is, "Do English usage and spelling count?" Usually they do, for the very good reason that writing is a major way to communicate our knowledge. In most subjects, it is difficult for the instructor to evaluate your knowledge unless you write using good grammar and spelling. Moreover, an important goal of a liberal arts education is to make people better communicators. A writing style like the one in the second sample betrays fuzzy thinking, a poor knowledge of English usage, and a general lack of familiarity with the topic. If knowledge and thoughts are well organized, the writing will likely reveal that. Also, it is not unfair to judge the quality of an essay on the basis of English usage in addition to subject content, because a college student should know English grammar. The student who wrote the second essay should have brought his or her writing skills up to a college level of competence before attempting other coursework. Regarding length, this was an essay test, not a short-answer test. The instructor specified that the essay should be at least three notebook-length pages. The second essay fell short by about 50 percent. (If your instructor does not specify the desired length for an essay, short-answer, definition test, and so forth, be sure to ask.) Other contrasts between the two sample tests follow:

1. Respondent one showed a comprehensive knowledge of the question and used material from the lectures and the books (a stated requirement). Respondent number two based his or her response mostly on lecture material. The little information drawn from books was presented in a way that showed a lack of understanding of that material.

2. Respondent one answered all parts of the question. Respondent two said nothing about the characteristics of animals compared to plants, for example.

3. Respondent one used a large portion of the specific vocabulary developed in the class and used it accurately. Respondent two used some of this vocabulary, but often inaccurately and misspelled.

4. Respondent two's logic was faulty. Consider his statement, "The vertebrates arose a boney fish. Having transformed its carbide plates into solidified bone." Vertebrates do not "arise" other organisms or "transform" themselves. They are not the agents of changes. The sentence should have read, "Some early vertebrates evolved into, or gave rise to, bony fish. The ancestral animal's skeleton was made of calcified cartilage. In bony fish, osteocytes (bone cells) evolved, and the mature animal's skeleton was now made up of bone along with some cartilage." The student's answer indicates the wrong causality. And the issue of evolutionary causality was a major topic in both the lecture and the books for the course.

A helpful device in writing essays is to assume that the reader (the professor or TA) has little knowledge of the topic. Even though this is a false assumption, it forces the student to write clearly, explain terms, and write in an organized manner. Your instructors should not have to guess what you know; they should be able to see it in your writing. Respondent one used this strategy (although not consistently), as illustrated by the following examples:

1. Respondent one wrote, "Animals cannot synthesize their food . . . " and then explained this statement by adding, ". . . but must ingest other organisms."
2. Respondent one used parentheses or dependent clauses to define or explain further, as in ". . . dorsal to it (in back of it) . . . "
3. Respondent one used phrases such as "that is" as in "Mammals are homiothermal. That is, their body temperature is constant."

Some printed sources that provide advice for taking tests are as follows:

Tesselman-Turkel, Judi, and Franklynn Peterson. *Test-Taking Strategies.* Madison: University of Wisconsin Press, 2004.

Fry, Ron. *"Ace" Any Test*, 5th ed. Clifton Park, NY: Thomson Delmar Learning, 2004.

Here are some resources that give general information on taking tests as well as information on taking specific types of tests:

"Taking Tests" at www.eiu.edu/~lrnasst/tests.htm

"How to Do Your Best on College Exams: Tips & Techniques for Before, During, and After" (from The College Board) at www.collegeboard.com/article/0,3868,2-10-0-962,00.html

Using the Library

The casual user of a library may only need to know how to use the online catalog and where to find the magazines, but a student doing research for a term paper or other project should have a more comprehensive knowledge of the library. Consequently, some colleges offer a course in library research methods. This individualized and sometimes self-paced course is highly recommended. Instruction on library use, plus experience, could make you an expert researcher. Knowing how to use the library can

Knowing how to use the library can make the difference between 10 productive hours in the library or 20 unproductive hours.

make the difference between spending 10 productive hours there or 20 unproductive hours. Also, collect any brochures or booklets on using the library that are distributed by the library. A very brief summary of the types of materials and resources available follows:

Librarians

Perhaps the most important resources at a library are the librarians! Do not hesitate to ask questions and seek advice from librarians. One of the main reasons that they are there is to help students. Do not be shy.

The Catalog

The old way of looking for books involved using a card catalog. Some libraries may still use this system or at least have it available for those who wish to use it. However, almost all schools have eliminated card catalogs and replaced them with online catalogs. The card catalog lists the books in the library on cards in a series of small filing cabinet–type drawers. Usually there are at least two catalogs, one listing books by author and title and the other by subject. Online catalogs not only tell you whether your library has a specific book, but they often indicate whether it is in the library or checked out. This saves you the time of having to go to the shelves to determine whether it is available. Libraries that are part of a network of libraries may have computer systems that allow you to search for books in any of the associated libraries. If you find a book that you would like to see and it is in an associated library, you can usually order it. It may take a few days to get it.

Other Library Resources

Today, many of the library resources traditionally found in printed material are online. However, subscriptions to online resources can be expensive. The number of online resources that your library subscribes to will depend on the college's budget for the library. You will have access to your library's databases through your student ID number or through passwords that you get from the library. You will be able to use the databases at the library or from home. Some of the library resources that might be available to you either in printed form or online are as follows:

■ **Books in Print.** Other than the college catalog, a way to find books by specific authors or on specific topics is to look in *Books in Print*, which is usually available in the reference or reserve section of the library or online. If your library does not have a book listed in *Books in Print*, you can then try to find it at a different library.

■ **Dictionaries, encyclopedias, almanacs, atlases, gazetteers, and other reference resources.** These types of materials often provide good starting points for a project. An encyclopedia article may give you a concise overview of a topic that facilitates your understanding of more detailed information found in other sources. Of course, some encyclopedias are easier to understand than others. If you have difficulty with the *Encyclopedia Britannica*, try something like the *World Book Encyclopedia*. There are also specialized encyclopedias that you might wish to consult for various subjects such as education, animals, art, philosophy, and science and technology, to name a few. Almanacs are annual publications containing facts and information on numerous topics. Atlases are collections of maps, and gazetteers are alphabetic listings of places with information about those places.

■ **Book review indexes and plot summaries.** If you are writing a book review or report, you may wish to consult one of the numerous book review indexes or plot summaries. Book review indexes tell you where to look for reviews of books. Some of them, such as *Book Review Digest*, also provide brief excerpts of book reviews. Plot summaries, such as *Masterplots*, give summaries of books, rather than reviews. Both book review indexes and plot summaries are useful tools, but they cannot replace your reading of the book in question. Indexes and summaries of plays, concerts, and films are also available. A reference librarian can help you find the source that fits your needs.

■ **Biographies.** Biographies provide information on people. Book-length biographies can be found in the college catalog. Shorter works can be found in the *Biography Index*. It lists biographical material in books that are not themselves biographies and also biographies that are found in periodicals. *Current Biography* is a set of volumes that give short sketches of living people. There are numerous other biographical resources in the library including various *Who's Who* books. Again, many of these sources can be found online. In addition, you can simply use a search engine to find information on almost anyone whom you would be researching.

■ **Pamphlets.** Libraries usually have government and other types of pamphlets available as well as online government resources. The pamphlet file often includes maps as well as informational booklets on virtually any topic.

■ **Periodicals.** Libraries also stock magazines and journals. To find information in periodicals, you must learn how to use the various computerized databases. There are general indexes, such as the Academic Search Elite (EBSCO) and Infotrak, and more than 200 specific ones, such as the Art Index. Indexes to numerous newspapers are also available. In many cases, online indexes will give you the complete text of an article or academic paper.

■ **Ebooks and etexts.** Your library might subscribe to one or more online databases that give you access to books and poetry. Books might include general fiction, textbooks, general nonfiction, reference books of all kinds, and anthologies. The databases might be very broad, providing thousands of titles, or very specific, providing a limited number of titles.

■ **Data, statistics, and the geographic information system.** These resources provide information on a variety of subjects. Some examples of resources that your library might subscribe to are *International Archive of*

Education Data, International Financial Statistics Online Service, Social Science Electronic Data Library, World Bank E-Library, Human Relations Area File (information on hundreds of different cultures), and *Commodity Trade Statistics Database (COMTRADE).* A valuable statistical database that is available without subscription is *Statistical Abstract of the United States* (www.census.gov/statab/www/).

It takes no computer literacy to use the simpler systems, and libraries have printed instructions on how to use the more complicated databases. Ask your librarian for help if you have trouble with the instructions.

If your college library does not have much in the way of computerized data banks, it might be worthwhile to find out if other libraries in your area do. These data banks can save hours of work compared to using printed indexes and often they lead to discoveries of important sources for which you were not even looking.

How to Find Information Using an Electronic Database or a Search Engine

Finding information on electronic databases such as Academic Search Elite (EBSCO), Education Resources Information Center (ERIC), and Infotrak or a search engine such as Google or Yahoo! takes skill. Here are some basic pointers:

1. **Use quotation marks.** If you are searching for an item that is described by more than one word, put the item in quotation marks. For instance, if you are looking for information on the topic language learning, type in *"language learning"*. Otherwise, every incidence of the word *language* and the word *learning* will be displayed in the results of your search.

2. **Use synonyms or change the order of words to conduct new searches.** For instance, if you are not satisfied with the results of your search under *"language learning"*, try *"language acquisition"*. Or, rearrange the words to *"learning language"* or *"acquisition language"*.

3. **Learn how to narrow your search.** If your search yields too many items for you to go through, narrow the search. For instance, if *"language learning"* resulted in thousands of hits, then type in what you are more specifically interested in researching, such as *"second language learning"*.

4. **Use key words.** If you cannot remember the exact name of something you wish to research, do a key word search (if available) using whatever word or words relating to the topic you can remember.

5. **Avoid wordiness.** Instead of entering in the search box *"How do people learn a second language"* enter *"second language learning"*. Usually prepositions, conjunctions, and articles do not need to be included in a search.

6. **Be specific.** If you are interested in second language learning in adults, enter the following: *"second language learning adults"*. Again, do not be wordy and also use as specific a word or words as possible. That is, do not use *"older people"* or *"people over the age of 18"* instead of the word *adult*. Also, notice that the word *adult* is outside the quotation marks. If it were inside, the search would yield only sources that used the exact sequence of words in the quotation marks. By leaving the word *adult* outside the quotation marks, the search will result in every instance in which *"second language learning"* occurs along with the word *adult*, regardless of how the word *adult* is used in the reference.

7. **Read the search instructions of whatever search engine or database you are using.** For instance, Google has a detailed tutorial on how to use its search engine that you can reach by clicking on "About Google" and then going to "Help and How to Search." Google also has pages called "Google Web Search Features" and "Google Services and Tools."

Writing Reports and Papers

Some beginning students put a fair amount of effort into finding out which instructors do not require written reports (term papers, book reports, field reports, laboratory reports, and so forth). This is a mistake in strategy. Ultimately, most students will have to write papers. Indeed, in some upper-division and graduate-level courses, a paper often is the total basis on which the instructor evaluates a student's performance. Thus, beginning students should place priority on honing their skills in this area as soon as possible. Some schools even offer a course in report writing. Ask your counselor if he or she recommends that you take such a course.

Preparing to Write

It is beyond the scope of this book to provide specific instruction for writing papers, but here is a list of suggestions that will help prepare you for writing assignments.

1. **Fulfill your English language requirements during your freshman and sophomore years.** It makes little sense to put this off because you "don't like English classes," or you are afraid of what your performance will be. *Writing skills are essential for students to succeed.* Putting off English classes until your junior or senior year may result in lower grades in other classes.

2. **Go to a writing lab or get a tutor.** Many schools provide walk-in writing labs or tutors to give students individual instruction. Usually, any registered student can use the lab for help in writing regardless of his or her major. Although you may not be enrolled in an English class, you can receive instruction in writing reports for any other class. Unlike tutors, lab instructors are professionals trained to assist you in the following areas:

- organization of papers
- sentence and paragraph structure
- grammar, punctuation, and spelling
- documentation of research papers
- building of self-confidence in writing

Some writing labs provide numerous free handouts on specific writing problems or have their own online information and tutorials.

3. **Read a book or two on writing.** This will give you more confidence, as well as improve your skills.

4. **Find out the specific requirements of each of your instructors.** One instructor may require a footnote style as outlined by the Modern Language Association (MLA), whereas another may prefer a completely different style. Some instructors may call for a straightforward reporting of facts but others may require your opinions. Make sure you know what your instructor wants before you begin a project.

5. **As with studying for tests, do not procrastinate.** Even the most experienced writer may have a hard time "getting into" a project. If you wait until the last week or a few days before a paper is due, you may not have enough time to develop the topic.

Tips to Follow When Writing

Follow these steps when preparing a paper:

1. **Choose a topic.** Unless your instructor has given you a limited number of choices, this task may require a considerable amount of thought. Do not choose a topic that requires specialized knowledge that you do not possess and

do not have enough time to acquire. Do not choose a topic that is too broad. One of the most common problems that students have is narrowing a topic down so that it is manageable. If you have the option to do so, choose a topic that interests you personally. You can look ahead in the textbook to get ideas, or in an initial trip to the library, look through magazines and journals for ideas. Do a survey in the library to determine whether there is enough information on the topic that you have chosen to support a paper of the required length. If the available information is inadequate, choose another topic.

2. **Check the topic you choose with the instructor.** He or she might tell you that your choice is not relevant to the course, that it is too broad in scope, or that it is too technical. Also, your instructor might be able to guide you to specific sources for your paper.

3. **Create a preliminary outline of your paper.** How is the paper going to be organized? What are you going to emphasize? If your instructor is willing to look at your preliminary outline and discuss your approach to the topic, take advantage of this. In fact, if the instructor is willing to look at the paper at various stages of its development and give you feedback, following any advice given by the instructor should greatly improve your chance of getting a good grade on the project.

4. **Choose an organizational structure.** How are you going to present the information—as a narrative (story-telling technique), a newspaper report, or some other style? Are you going to give more than one point of view on your topic or just your own?

5. **Do more detailed library research.** (See the previous section on using the library.) It is important to keep track of the sources from which you get your information. As you take notes, clearly write down all the bibliographic information. For books, also write down call numbers, the numbers and letters placed at the spine of the books and used to locate them in the library. This way you can easily relocate the book. For Internet sites write down the URL.

6. **Consider using interviews as one source of information.** For instance, if you are doing a report on an academic topic, the faculty of your college or university might be a resource. Find out if anyone on campus is an expert on the topic that you have chosen for your paper. If so, ask that person to talk to you about his or her work. If there are no experts on campus, find out the names of experts from written sources, by asking instructors, or through an Internet search. Email or call these individuals and ask if you could interview them online or by phone.

7. **Use only valid sources.** Clarify this with your instructor. Most instructors would not consider the *National Enquirer* to be a legitimate source

of information. Because they are not primary sources, *Time, Newsweek,* and other similar publications may also be considered unsuitable.

8. **Except for background reading, use the most recent data that are available.** A report on human genetics, for instance, based on sources that are even a year old might be "dated."

9. **After you have enough data, begin to write your paper by expanding your preliminary outline.** Then you can convert each segment of the outline, one by one, into good prose. After you have written an initial draft, carefully go over it for spelling and grammatical problems. Look for internal inconsistencies and problems in logic.

10. **Have someone read the paper and ask him or her to make constructive comments and corrections.** Even experienced writers often have copy editors who proofread their manuscripts. Have a friend, parent, tutor, or writing laboratory instructor read your paper. As mentioned earlier, sometimes the instructor to whom the paper will be submitted will give you comments on a preliminary draft. Studying the comments that other people make about your paper will provide you with a good learning experience—about writing in general as well as the subject matter of the paper.

11. **Write the final draft and proofread it.** Some instructors do not allow any typographical errors or obvious mistakes. Make sure you know your instructor's policy in regard to this.

Dartmouth University has an extensive section on its website on writing academic papers called "Writing the Academic Paper." It includes general information on writing reports and papers as well as specific sections on writing for the humanities, the social sciences, and the sciences, and on special writing tasks. You can visit the site at www.dartmouth.edu/~writing/materials/student/toc.shtml.

A Note on Plagiarism

Plagiarism is the act of representing other people's ideas, words, and/or data that they have collected as being the product of one's own effort. It is therefore a form of lying or cheating. Sometimes, of course, it results from a person not knowing the rules by which the originator of information or ideas should be given credit. Even so, if discovered, plagiarism in college is likely to be treated as a major offense. The punishment for students may range from receiving a failing grade on a particular paper to being excluded from a class to receiving a failing grade in the course. In some universities, plagiarism might result in expulsion from the school. Some instructors have access to software that can check a student's paper for plagiarism.

The way to avoid plagiarism is to use liberally footnotes or other methods of citing sources. Different instructors will prescribe different methods of noting references. Always give sources for the following:

1. Direct quotes.

2. Paraphrased material. (Even if you put another person's ideas into your own words, you should give that person credit.)

3. Data that are the result of someone's research.

Credit for material from any source, written or not, must be included. Oral sources, such as material gathered from lectures, television programs, or personal communications, must be credited. You do not have to cite sources for anything that has become common knowledge, such as Earth being the third planet from the sun.

With the increasing use of the Internet, the opportunities for purposeful or accidental plagiarism have increased. It is easy to download documents and paste them into a report that you are writing. If you do this or simply include data from an electronic source, you must cite it as you would a printed source. Individual instructors may have their own instructions on how to cite Internet sources. You can also consult the most recent edition of the *MLA Handbook for Writers of Research Papers* (New York, Modern Language Association of America) for the MLA's guides to citations or check Yahoo's "Writing for the Web" at http://dir.yahoo.com/Social_Science/communications/Writing/writing_for_the_web/.

Instructors seldom expect lower-division term papers or projects to be based on original research or concepts. Instead, these papers are meant to show how the student can collect information, organize that information, and present it in a logical and well-written manner. Thus, it is expected that you give proper citations to the information presented.

Critical Thinking

In 1987, several books that were highly critical of the American educational system were published. All became national best-sellers. These books are:

- Bloom, Allan. *The Closing of the American Mind—How Higher Education Has Failed Democracy and Impoverished the Souls of Today's Students.* New York: Simon & Schuster, 1987.

- Hirsch, E. D., Jr. *Cultural Literacy.* Boston: Houghton Mifflin, 1987.
- Boyer, Ernest. *College: The Undergraduate Experience in America.* New York: Harper & Row, 1987.

These books dealt with a wide range of concerns, but an underlying theme was that American schools teach skills rather than information, and that they attempt to teach students how to make a living rather than how to think. According to the authors of these books, American students generally lack the ability to form broad insights about information and to analyze that information intellectually. Although the authors were in turn themselves criticized for simplistic thinking on many points, their ideas have had an impact on the American educational system. Critical thinking is being emphasized today throughout the nation's schools. *Critical thinking* can be defined as the mental processes used to make judgments about the truth or merit of concepts and data.

When you write papers and take essay examinations, you should attempt to do more than "regurgitate" material that you have read or heard in a lecture, unless that was specifically asked of you. Depending on the question or topic, you may wish to compare, contrast, criticize, synthesize, give an overview, analyze the meaning of, argue an opposing view, find an underlying meaning, or propose a novel opinion or idea. However, it takes knowledge and an understanding of logic to do these tasks.

Many colleges and universities require one or more courses in critical thinking. These courses may be found in a number of departments, including but not limited to philosophy, linguistics, mathematics, and English. Because many instructors in all disciplines are increasingly asking their students to display critical thinking abilities, it would be wise to learn these methods early in your college career. Along with English language courses and basic math classes, a course in logic should be taken in the freshman year.

There is much more to critical thinking than I have discussed, and it is beyond the scope of this guide to teach critical thinking. However, some practical suggestions can be offered:

1. **When taking lecture notes, write down any questions that you have about the data.** Indicate any information that does not seem to correspond with information you have previously heard or read. Ask the instructor about such inconsistencies.

2. **When reading a textbook, ask questions about the material and check out inconsistencies between the text and the lecture**

material. Also, ask yourself if the author might have left out significant information, not discussed alternative explanations, used statistics incorrectly, or used ambiguous phrases. The only way you can make these judgments is by being trained in critical thinking and by being motivated enough to investigate, with research, any possible problems in an author's presentation.

3. **When studying for a test, anticipate possible questions and carefully think out your answers.** The worst time to attempt to think analytically or creatively is during a test—when there is time pressure and often a general feeling of nervousness.

4. **Study in groups.** Ask other students their ideas on the subject in question. Debate positions with them. Validate ideas and information that they offer by consulting textbooks or other sources that your instructor has judged to be competent.

These suggested activities will help you to develop critical thinking skills. However, to engage in them properly you may need the formal training that will equip you with the abilities and techniques to ask relevant and important questions, to judge inconsistencies, to make judgments about the honesty and degree of bias of a person's claims, to determine whether mathematical or statistical evidence is being used correctly, to anticipate test questions, and to argue a position.

One of the goals of a liberal arts education is to prepare citizens to analyze what they hear and read about politics, economics, morality, ethics, social relationships, products, and everyday affairs in a logical and insightful manner. Critical thinking is a tool of daily life, not just a set of abstract skills for use in a classroom.

Before you take a course in logic or even before you take your first college courses, you may wish to read a book on critical thinking. Five easily readable books on critical thinking, even for a person with no previous formal exposure to the topic, follow. The first four books teach the basic tools of general logic and problem solving; the fifth specifically refers to logic as used in social science.

Missimer, Connie A. *Good Argument: An Introduction to Critical Thinking*, 4th ed. Englewood Cliffs, NJ: Prentice Hall, 2005.

Conway, David A., Ronald Munson, and Andrew Black. *The Elements of Reasoning*, 4th ed., Belmont, CA: Wadsworth, 2004.

Paul, Richard, and Linda Elder. *Critical Thinking: Learn the Tools the Best Thinkers Use,* Concise ed. Englewood Cliffs, NJ: Prentice Hall, 2006.

Potter, James W. *Becoming a Strategic Thinker: Developing Skills for Success.* Englewood Cliffs, NJ: Prentice Hall, 2005.

Hoover, Kenneth R., and Todd Donovan. *The Elements of Social Scientific Thinking*, 8th ed. Belmont, CA: Wadsworth, 2004.

Also see Critical Thinking on the Web, a website with numerous links to tutorials and other information on critical thinking. The address is www.austhink.org/critical/.

Outside the College Walls

Education and Travel

The purpose of a college education is to create a worldly and knowledgeable person who can make rational and informed decisions. The classroom experience can take you only so far toward this goal. Foreign travel can take you closer to meeting this goal. Only through actual contact with cultures different from your own can you begin to break down ethnocentric beliefs and emotions. Most colleges offer travel courses through their regular schedules of classes or through extension classes. Many universities have arrangements with foreign universities and allow students to spend a semester or more of study at those foreign universities. These foreign programs are highly recommended, especially to general liberal arts and social science students. See your college catalog or student advisor for information on your school's international studies programs. One major university with such a program can be viewed at www.international.ucla.edu/centers.asp.

If you sign up for any international studies program run by a private company, confirm that it is an accredited and reputable company and a known entity to teaching faculty, counselors, or administrators at your college. Verify all of the claims it makes in advertisements and seek advice from the proper people at your college about its program.

Career Planning and Getting a Job

Career planning and getting a job are complex activities, and a detailed treatment of these subjects is not possible in this brief guide. Instead, I will provide you with some basic facts and ideas and suggest some sources that offer detailed treatment of the topics.

First, maintain a high GPA. As discussed in the section on the consequence of low grades in Chapter 2, the importance of grades once you have
left school varies. However, getting passable grades is important to progress
from one level of a course of study to the next. If you get a low grade in an
undergraduate class, you may have to repeat it before you can take the next
course in a sequence of courses. This could extend your time at school. For
job seeking, a GPA will be more or less important depending on the job
and the employer. For science, engineering, and other technically oriented
jobs, high grades may be essential. For teaching jobs, especially at the
college or university level, grades may also be very important. Of course, if
one goes into business for oneself, even as a doctor, a lawyer, a consultant,

For science, engineering, and other technically
oriented jobs, high grades may be essential.

a politician, or a business owner, grades may have little or no importance. For example, in 2005, *Time Magazine* (June 20, 2005, p. 21) reported that both George W. Bush and his 2004 challenger for president of the United States, John Kerry, graduated with middle C GPAs.

Second, begin planning your career a long time before you graduate. Here are several suggestions for doing so:

1. **Join one or more professional organizations that correspond to your major and/or minor.** (See "List of Scholarly Organizations" in Appendix B.) Being a member of such an organization, and, better yet, participating in some of its activities potentially will provide you with valuable academic information that you did not get in the classroom and in some cases will allow you to gain practical experience in your chosen field. Membership in professional organizations may also provide you with important future contacts. Academic organizations often have their own job listings and employment departments. There are fees to join a professional organization. Student membership fees are usually considerably less than those of full-time professionals. If your field offers more than one professional organization, talk to your professors and department advisor about which organization(s) would be best for you to join.

2. **Apply for internships or do volunteer work related to your area of study.** If possible apply for an internship or volunteer work at a place where you might wish to work after you graduate. This can sometimes be done with private corporations and also with government agencies such as the Department of Education, the Department of Energy, the Department of Human and Health Resources, the National Institutes of Health, the National Park Service, the Federal Bureau of Investigation, and virtually every other major government agency. See the federal internship's website at www.house.gov/bishop/FederalInternship.html.

Employers often ask applicants to have a degree and job experience. Internships can provide valuable job experience and practical skills. They can also give students experience with their chosen career. That experience may reinforce students' interest or direct them to look elsewhere for a career. For example, a person wishing to become a doctor who works in some capacity in a hospital may be inspired by the work or dislike it so much that the person changes his or her career goal. Check with your academic department or college career office for a list of possible internships.

Internships and volunteer work are often done during summer breaks, although there are many exceptions to this. For instance, at the college where I work, the Los Angeles sheriff's department polices the campus. The sheriff's department has a year-round intern (cadet) program for people interested in law enforcement.

3. **If you cannot find an internship for which you qualify, look for a part-time job in your field of study.** Sometimes those jobs can be found at your school. You may apply for jobs as a lab assistant, teaching assistant, tutor, or any type of student worker. This not only gives you experience in your area of interest, but it allows you to build a network of relationships that might be helpful later.

4. **Join a club or another student organization that deals with your career aspirations.** Membership in such groups not only looks good on a resume, but it provides you with experience in your area of interest and often exposure to professionals in the field you wish to enter.

5. **Network.** This step is crucial and should be done by every college student. Your supervisor for a college job, internship, or volunteer work, as well as the sponsor for a college club or people you meet through a professional organization, might have ideas or even connections that might help you get a job after you graduate. Even other students in your major who have connections might be able to use those connections to help you.

6. **Learn how to write an effective resume.** The resume often is the first information that a potential employer uses to evaluate you. It needs to set you apart from other applicants and be worded correctly or it might be the last thing the potential employer knows about you. Find out whether your college career office has information on resume writing or whether personal development courses that cover this important practical topic are available at your college.

In addition to visiting your college's career and jobs office, you might want to visit the following Internet sites. Many sites charge a fee for their use. I have provided only a small sample of the job and career sites available. You can do your own Internet search for other sites. Check with a school career counselor to see if he or she has recommendations as to which site might be most useful to you.

Welcome to MyRoad™, The College Board's college career website at http://apps.collegeboard.com/myroad/navigator.jsp.

Career and College Planning Resources has numerous links not only to career planning but also to most topics relating to college. It can be found at www.khake.com/page51.html.

CollegeView offers information on career planning, job searches, and resume writing at www.collegeview.com.

Quintessential Careers at www.quintcareers.com/.

The U.S. Department of Labor, Bureau of Labor Statistics. This site provides *The Occupational Outlook Handbook.* The address is www.bls.gov/oco/.

If your career center does not have a list of Internet sources relating to jobs and careers, consult Career Services. This is a site produced by the Alumni Association of the University of California, Santa Barbara. It can be found at www.ucsbalum.com/career_services/jobsearch/links.html.

Giving Out Your Personal Information

It is important to investigate the ethical practices of the companies that provide job and career services. This is, of course, true for your dealings with any company. One thing that should immediately send up a red flag is when a business (on the Internet or otherwise) asks you for personal numbers such as Social Security numbers and student identification numbers when these numbers are not necessary to conduct the business. Unscrupulous people can use this information to access your bank accounts and even to steal your identity. Identity theft is a relatively common crime (the Federal Trade Commission reported 635,000 cases of fraud and identity theft in 2004) and students are not immune to it.

Typical business transactions are unlikely to require a Social Security number or other numbers tied into your personal information or monetary accounts. Your school will most likely want your Social Security number, as well as government agencies such as those to which you might apply for loans and grants. However, if you send personal information out over the Internet, make sure you are on a secure site. For instance, a website whose URL starts with "https" (as opposed to just "http") is supposed to be a secure site. Information on these sites is encrypted for security.

Do not conduct business that requires Social Security numbers, bank account numbers, or other numbers that could be used to access important personal information on networked computers. Personal identification numbers (PINS) and other access numbers could be retrieved by someone and used to steal your personal information. Networked computers include computers that are available to students in libraries and computer labs.

Also protect your PINS and passwords. For instance, do not keep passwords in your wallet with the cards that need those passwords. Thieves will try every number they find with each card. Do not share your PINS and passwords with friends. In regard to credit cards, most security experts say that you should not use them in instances when they are taken away from you to process, such as in restaurants.

Protecting oneself from fraud is a complex matter in the information age. I can only provide some basic suggestions here. For much more comprehensive information on identity theft and other security issues see the following websites:

ED.gov, the U.S. Department of Education's site on security matters for students, at www.ed.gov/about/offices/list/oig/misused/index.html

ID Thief Statistics at www.consumer.gov/idtheft

Consumer Protection at http://sls.rutgers.edu/consumer_protection.htm

Vocabulary Building

A common complaint from students is, "Do we have to know all those terms?" Although words used every day might sometimes be sufficient substitutes for more technical terms, they often are not. Usually a technical term used by a classroom professor or found in a text defines a concept more precisely than a corresponding common word. For instance, a biology instructor may refer to a dog as *Canis familiaris.* To those who have learned its meaning, this term conveys more information than "dog." By naming the species, a significant amount of information about the relationship of a dog (*Canis familiaris*) to other species is revealed. For example, since all species named *Canis* are closely related to each other, one can tell that *Canis familiaris* is closely related to *Canis lupis* (the wolf). The point of this discussion is not biological classification, but to illustrate how a technical term encodes more specific information than its common-word equivalent. Some technical terms, of course, do not even have a close equivalent in common usage.

Vocabulary words used in a college course may have a different meaning from a common usage. For instance, the word *status* as used in social science refers to a person's position in society relative to other positions. It does not necessarily refer to an exalted position, as in "My father has a lot of status because he is the president of a large corporation." All positions are statuses in the sociological sense. "Father" is a status, as is "mother," "student," "teacher," "doctor," "nurse," "employer," and "employee." Be careful to learn the specialized meaning of words that are also in common usage so that you do not confuse the two meanings.

Here are some suggestions to build your vocabulary:

1. **Do not ignore unfamiliar words.** If these words occur during a lecture, raise your hand and ask what they mean; otherwise you might not understand part of the lecture. If they are in a book, newspaper, or magazine, look them up in a dictionary or glossary. Doing so immediately may clarify a whole sentence or topic.

2. **Work on general vocabulary building.** The best way to accomplish this is by doing a lot of reading and following suggestion 1—look up all the words you do not know. A faster way of building vocabulary is to purchase one of the numerous vocabulary-building books available in any large bookstore and set a goal of learning a specific number of words each day. Make flash cards to help you remember the words. Put one word on one side of a card, and on the reverse side put the definitions along with an example or two of the word as it is used in sentences. This last step is very important, because words should always be learned in the context of their usage.

3. **Learn Latin and Greek affixes and roots.** More than 90 percent of English's scientific and technological vocabulary is derived from Latin and Greek. About 60 percent of general English words are derived directly or indirectly from Latin or Greek. For instance, *malus* is the Latin word that means "evil" or "bad." It is used in such words as *malpractice, malice, maladjusted, malcontent,* and *malediction.* The element *dico-* means to "speak," and a *malediction* is a curse.

Another example can be given using a Greek root and an affix. For instance, the word *anonymous* is made up of two Greek elements, *an-,* meaning "not," and *onyma,* meaning "name." *Anonymous* refers to a person whose name is not known.

Over time, words change in meaning, so the current meaning of a word may not be completely apparent from its Latin or Greek elements. Yet, the current meaning of numerous English words (perhaps 50,000 or more) is close to the Latin or Greek elements from which they are composed. Thus, knowing these elements is a great vocabulary-building device.

Based on one of the books listed on the next page or a similar book, construct a list that includes the most common Latin and Greek affixes and roots. Write each entry on an index card with its meaning and examples of its use on the back of the card. Keep these cards with you so you can study them during idle times, such as on a bus, between classes, or on a work break.

The meaning of Latin and Greek elements can be found in the following books:

- Green, Tamara M. *The Greek and Latin Roots of English*, 3rd ed. Lanham, MD: Rowman & Littlefield, 2004.

- Lundquist, Joegil K., and Jeanne L. Lundquist. *English from the Roots of Greek, Latin: Help for Reading, Writing, Spelling and S.A.T. Scores.* Medina, WA: Literacy Unlimited Publications, 2004.

- Ayers, Donald. *English Words from Latin and Greek Elements.* Tucson: University of Arizona Press, 1986.

Additional Sources of Information

Websites on Preparing for College and Study Skills

- **The U.S. Department of Education** has an excellent website on preparing for, choosing, applying for, funding for, and attending college. The website also has a section on repaying student loans. The web address is http://studentaid.ed.gov/PORTALSwebApp/students/english/index.jsp.

- **Preparing for College: An Online Tutorial** is from the University of Washington. This is a site with extensive links to other resources on most topics covered in this book. It is found at www.washington.edu/doit/Brochures/Academics/cprep.html.

- **CollegePrep-101** is a site from Oklahoma State University College of Education: http://collegeprep.okstate.edu/.

- **Mapping Your Future** has general information on financing college, career planning, selecting a college, and other information relevant to college students. It is found at www.mapping-your-future.org/.

Companies That Provide Resources

This section lists companies that produce one or more series of books, software, or other resources that are designed to aid students. Most of these resources are available to buy in neighborhood bookstores, from online booksellers, or from the publisher. A web address is provided for each company. Each company's home page provides a detailed catalog of its products and services. You will also be able to check out many of these items from a library.

Be careful in your use of self-help books on specific academic subjects. They are meant to supplement and clarify, not replace, the information you receive in class and from your textbooks. Investigate any inconsistencies between a self-help book and other sources of information with your instructors. Also, make sure you check the copyright date. In some fields, such as biology, anthropology, and health, new discoveries are always being made and new interpretations of information are continually being postulated. Consequently, some of the information in a book that is just a couple of years old might be out of date.

Printed Materials and Software

■ **Barnes & Noble's SparkNotes** (www.sparknotes.com/). SparkNotes started as an independent online company and was bought by Barnes & Noble, Inc. Barnes & Noble publishes SparkNotes guides in book form. These books are brief reviews of numerous academic topics. All of the published book titles, plus others, are available online (see the following section). SparkNotes also publishes test preparation books, literature reviews, sets of flash cards on various topics, SparkCharts (charts that summarize the main terms and concepts for a variety of topics), and other educational products.

■ **Made Simple Books: Barron's Educational Series** (www.barrons-educ.com/). This company publishes more than 2000 educational books under various series names, such as *Easy Way*, *Study Keys*, and *Painless*.

■ **Research & Education Association** (www.rea.com). This is another company that publishes hundreds of review books, test preparation books, flash card books, examination notes in the form of charts, literature guides, language-learning books, and reference books.

■ **Greenhaven Press** (www.galegroup.com/greenhaven/). This press (now a division of Thomson Publishing) publishes nonfiction educational books on hundreds of topics. Its series of books includes *Opposing Viewpoints*. Each of these books examines a controversial topic, such as abortion, gun control, stem cell research, and hundreds of others, from various points of view. *Opposing Viewpoints* is also available online (see the next section).

Internet Resources

This section provides a list of Internet resources that were not mentioned in the body of the book. They represent a sample of the academic websites on the Internet. Anyone can create a web page and, therefore, the information that one finds on the Internet is often suspect. For that reason, this list is restricted to the websites of well-known educational products companies, universities, government sources, and respected institutions and organizations. This is not a guarantee of accuracy, but it decreases the chance that you are viewing information that has not been reviewed by people other than the originator of the material. Also, be sure to visit your college library home page. It might provide a more comprehensive list of Internet resources for students or simply different ones from those listed here.

■ **SparkNotes** (www.sparknotes.com). SparkNotes allows free on-screen access to many of its guides, but there is a fee to print them. Many of these guides on academic topics and test preparation are also available in book form and are published by Barnes & Noble (see previous section). There are hundreds of books on numerous topics. The literature reviews are especially numerous and cover recent fiction as well as classics. Remember, outlines or brief treatments of a topic are not meant to substitute for reading the assigned material in a class. Use them only to help you increase your understanding of the material.

■ **Research & Education Association** (www.rea.com) **and Barron's Educational Series** (www.barronseduc.com/). The REA website allows you to take short sample standardized tests such as the GRE, LSAT, and SAT for free. You have to subscribe (and pay a fee) to use the Barron's site, but it offers full-length practice tests.

■ **Brooks/Cole: Opposing Viewpoints Resource Center** (www.brookscole.com/pubco/serv_opposing.html). This site combines the resources of Greenhaven Press (see the previous section) with reference sources from Gale Publishing and Macmillan Publishing. It contains discussions and debates on most of the important issues discussed in the academic world. Find out if your college library or a neighborhood library subscribes to this site. Or, if you are currently using a textbook that is published by Thomson Publishing (it owns Greenhaven, Gale, and Macmillan), find out if that book provides you with a code that gives you limited-time access to the site. The site also has sections on critical thinking and writing a research paper.

- **Argumentative Essay Topics** (www.gc.maricopa.edu/english/topicarg.html). This site lists numerous essay topics. When you click on a topic, you are sent to a page with references to that topic.

- **International Debate Education Association (IDEA)** (www.debatabase.org/). This site lists about 300 topics and provides information and links for all of those topics.

- **Public Agenda** (www.publicagenda.org/issues/issuehome.cfm). This Internet service provides information on controversial topics and includes public opinion on each issue and links to further data.

List of Scholarly Organizations

The Scholarly Societies Project, at www.scholarly-societies.org, is maintained by the University of Waterloo Library. It provides a directory and links to hundreds of organizations, such as the American Anthropological Association, the College Art Association of America, and the American Institute of Biological Science, that might be useful to you. These organizational web pages have information on organizations' publications and conventions as well as information on their subject area and links to other sites. They can be useful in obtaining information for research papers. You may also wish to think about getting a student membership in an organization that deals with your major. Newsletters and other information and opportunities afforded by membership may increase your interest in your major as well as your motivation to go beyond classroom learning.

Index